Thoughtful Own

Canine Behavior and Training
A Triadic Approach

by
James Akenhead, Ed.D.

Certified Professional Dog Trainer, CCPDT
Certified Dog Behavior Consultant, IAABC
Certified Professional Trainer, OBCCS
Certified Dog Trainer, IABC

CCB Publishing
British Columbia, Canada

Thoughtful Owners, Great Dogs: Canine Behavior and Training
A Triadic Approach

Copyright ©2009 by James Akenhead
ISBN-13   978-1-926585-35-2
First Edition

Library and Archives Canada Cataloguing in Publication

Akenhead, James, 1943-
Thoughtful owners, great dogs : canine behavior and training : a triadic
approach / written by James Akenhead – 1st ed.
Includes bibliographical references.
ISBN 978-1-926585-35-2
1. Dogs--Training. 2. Dogs--Behavior. I. Title.
SF431.A34 2009   636.7'0887   C2009-903952-4

Publisher: CCB Publishing
             British Columbia, Canada
             www.ccbpublishing.com

Disclaimer

Consider the Liability Waiver in Section 9 of this book to be in effect for you as a reader. If you can not accept the waiver presented herein, do not continue reading. Finally; never do anything with your dog that seems risky or dangerous unless you have qualified first hand personal advice from a professional trainer or behavior worker.

14143 Ravenna Avenue
Alliance, Ohio 44601
Phone: 330-935-0186

bigdogs@neo.rr.com
www.signaturek9training.com

Signature K-9 Behavior & Training LLC

Dedication

To Journey (Front Cover) **and Blitz** (Back Cover)

Their Friends and Extended Family
Our Companions and Teachers

Buff, Johnny, Dozer, Sough, Sisca, Rex, Oakie,
Dutch, Wisdom, Duke, Nick, Diesel, Nikk,
Cowie, Skippy, Greta, Walker, Callie, Shaman,
Zoe, Shaningo, Allie, Kalick, Aris

And to Our Clients and Friends

With Special Thanks

Beth Heidi Adelman the editor who whipped this
book into shape, she kept after me to clarify my ideas.
She is bright, patient, and understanding,
a true professional in every way.

Paul Rabinovitch of CCB Publishing.
Artful in cover design, rich with perspective about the
literary world, and efficient in every step of production,
he makes the whole process enjoyable.

Contents

Section 1. Overview

The Triadic Approach

This book is not for dummies. You must be a thoughtful owner if you want a great dog. Dogs are not television sets. They are living beings. If you really want a good relationship, it takes thoughtful effort on your part.

As for the Triadic Approach, I like it because when you're writing a book, you're always looking for something that makes yours sound like it deserved to be written. In this case, the title fit perfectly. You see, the Triadic Approach, as explained by Drs. Jon Bailey and Mary Burch in their book *How to Think Like a Behavior Analyst,* is a perfect approach to helping thoughtful owners develop great relationships with their dog. The approach includes the following parts:

1. Professionally analyzing an animal's behavior and creating a plan for achieving a desired end.

2. Teaching and demonstrating for the dog's owner or handler how to understand the situation and use the plan to achieve a goal.

3. Supporting the owner with feedback and demonstrations while he or she works through a plan with the dog.

It's a 1, 2, 3 process. Analyze the behavior and make a plan, educate the owner about how to implement the plan, and support the owner-handler as she implements the plan. This is the nature of the process explained in this book. The emphasis is that the professional's role is to help the owner-handler understand behavior so she can work with her dog to reach the desired end.

Two Species, Two Components
In our version of this approach, there area two components. One involves humans, the other involves dogs. Both are equally important. Without attention to each of these primary components, effectiveness will be compromised. These components represent two very different entities… **two different species.** Recognizing this important fact enables us to appropriately attend to each.

Within each of these primary components, there are two factors that must be attended to in order to maximize success. One is accomplishing goals or tasks; the other is maintaining a relationship. Both of these must be focuses of attention for the human and the dog. I will do my best to address both.

My Approach
This book is written for pet dog owners. And it is with trepidation that I write it at all. That's because it seems the only thing two dog trainers can agree on is what a third one is doing wrong. You see, dog trainers and behavior consultants are in the constant throes of discussion or argument about what is good training and good science. Even those with advanced degrees have disagreements, sometimes including vehement arguments that produce hard feelings.

My approach will be to write just as I would talk to you if you were a client at our training facility. What I will cover represents the issues and concerns that show up most often. No book can cover every possible contingency. If you are a client, you will recognize this as an overview of what you have heard, along with some additional information that we may not have had time to discuss in your private consultation.

This is the model we use when building a base for positive human-canine relationships and to prevent future problems. This model is also used as a starting place when behavior problems have already surfaced. Once this model is in place, undesired behaviors are dealt with using a problem-solving process that takes into account the desires of the dog's owner and the realities of the dog's environment. Since I am not able to see your dog and personally advise you as to safety concerns, **if anything suggested here seems dangerous or risky to you, do not do it!** If you try a suggestion and run into trouble, I strongly recommend that you get help from a trainer or a behavior professional.

Client Concerns

Calls we receive encompass a wide range of problems. In this book, we include information on the questions that we hear most often. If you find that the guidance given does not help to resolve your problems, you should contact a dog trainer or a behavior consultant. Some situations require specific problem-solving strategies or a good management plan. Suggestions about what to consider if you need help are offered in our section on selecting a dog trainer.

In the world of dog behavior and training, things are

changing all the time. New information comes to the forefront as new research is done. If you question something here or something you are told by a trainer, get a second opinion. There are many paths to solving a problem. My biggest proviso is that if your second opinion suggests a punitive approach, get a third opinion. Punishment is very tricky to manage; it should not be used indiscriminately, and especially not by one who does not fully understand the principles of operant and classical conditioning.

Personal Orientation

Core beliefs: The following are beliefs that drive my behavior and training work:

- I believe there is a force greater than me.

- I believe I am not capable of fully understanding this force or how it works.

- I suspect this force is involved in relationships between humans and dogs.

- I believe that life is precious and dignity is due to all life.

- I agree with the premise Do No Harm.

- I believe the definition of harm is tied to one's belief structure.

Once the relationship is established, the focus is on behavior. To psychoanalyze a dog does little good. The real task is to identify unwanted behaviors, find triggers and devise plans to change behavior. In this pursuit, I accept that behavior is not linear. When working with difficult problems, sometimes breakthroughs occur when you least expect them; other times, it seems like progress occurs at a crawl.

A graph that starts where a problem is identified and ends where a solution is achieved is not a straight line. It is represented by ups, downs and plateaus, much like a stock chart. As we deal with these ups and downs, we must remain positive.

Research Is Valuable

Good research shows us the way in many cases. But because of the expense involved in conducting research, it is often incomplete. In the absence of clear research results, experience and the intuition of knowledgeable trainers and behavior professionals must be used, as long as they stay within a positive training orientation.

Black Swans

A black swan is an unknown, inconceivable event. Black swan events can cause substantial unanticipated change. Black swans remind us that no matter how smart we think we are, we don't know everything. There is always more to come.

Personal Models

I use a personal model in all my work (see *Unless You Are a Hermit: Success Means Working with People*, 2008). I believe in establishing processes or protocols for doing things and then analyzing success to determine what changes need to be made in those processes. I believe that life is about planning and solving problems. Some of those problems have a tangible basis and some are based on values. Those that are value-based are often more difficult to deal with. Much of the relationship between people and dogs is value-based.

Writing Style
Informal will be the style used here. "We" will be used some of the time when referring to what goes on. This is because, in most cases, no one does it alone. I have great support from my wife, Dr. Charlene Akenhead, as well as other consultants, trainers and veterinarians we call upon.

In some cases, my explanations may seem too detailed. I do this because I don't want to assume that those reading are on the same page as I am. Without details, we are left to make up what goes on. That is when our imagination may totally change the intended meaning. I apologize for instances where I fall short in my attempt to make things clear.

About Learning
As you go through this book, you will be introduced to some new ideas and skills for working with your dog. One factor that will contribute to your success is a willingness to stick to it when it feels weird. When we learn new information or try new skills, there may be a period when they seem uncomfortable. New ideas may go against previously ingrained beliefs. New skills, even simple ones, can seem awkward when first used.

As we learn new ways to work with our dogs, we go through predictable stages. These stages are the same ones we go through when we learn to play tennis, water ski or shift an automobile's manual transmission. Getting a handle on these stages can help us understand why new things can sometimes feel so uncomfortable.

Blissful Ignorance

This is the starting point. This is when we're not yet aware of the new information or of how it will feel to practice new skills. We don't yet have reason to be uncomfortable. It might be like when we became old enough to drive a car and had to learn on a manual transmission.

At first, it's all about what learning to drive can do for us. Then comes the realization that there are three pedals on the floor and we only have two feet. Next, we realize that we only have two hands and there are at least three things we might be required to use them for. At this point, some of us even wonder how a human being can be expected to carry out all of these activities with only two arms and two legs. The irony here is that such thoughts may surface even though thousands of people are successful at the endeavor that is giving us trouble.

I'm Uncomfortable

When first introduced to new ideas and skills, many come to grips with the fact that they don't really understand how to use them. That awareness can cause discomfort. Based on a person's natural operating style, some skills will come more naturally than others.

The discomfort experienced while learning new skills is as

much a part of the natural learning process as it was the first time you learned to do math or speak a foreign language. It is in this stage that some give up rather than take time to practice or risk being embarrassed as rough spots get worked out.

I've Got It

A third phase occurs when we can apply concepts and skills, but that application takes concentration. In this stage, it's like learning to play golf or tennis. You've got to keep your eye on the ball as well as concentrate on the grip and swing you've been taught.

In this phase of learning, things often feel unnatural. The skill has not yet become an integral part of our style. When you notice this weird feeling, just remember, even though it feels odd, it will still work just fine.

Smooth and Integrated

The final stage of learning is when once clumsy, difficult skills and concepts become automatic. In this stage of learning, the skills and related concepts are so integrated that there is no longer a need to consciously think about them. They occur naturally, as circumstances dictate. It's like jumping into your car, starting it, putting it in gear, letting out the clutch, pushing the gas pedal, turning on the turn signal and rolling down the road—all without a conscious awareness of what is happening.

Refinement

Much like when a seasoned athlete must learn new plays, some of these learning stages will recur when a skill refinement is added. It might be like the small adjustment you must make when switching from a four-speed to a five-speed manual shift in your car. You experience a few minor grinds, but no big problem. In this context, it's good to consider that if no discomfort is ever felt, growth may not be taking place.

Section 2. Before You Start Training

Professional Trainers and Behaviorists

There is no single national or state agency for licensing or certifying dog trainers or behavior professionals and there are no uniform certification standards. Various universities, specialty schools and other organizations provide programs and certify graduates. Methods vary greatly. Because there is no uniform trainer certification standard, anyone can declare him or herself a dog trainer. Because no standard exists, it's important to carefully consider the credentials of those you may choose as guides for you and your dog.

Many well-meaning people advertise themselves as dog trainers. Of those, some are members of training clubs. In those clubs, a trainer may come from the ranks of the membership and their credentials may rest on the fact that they and their own dogs have earned titles. Add to those former K-9 (that is, working dog) trainers and self-appointed dog disciplinarians, as well as those who believe they have a special relationship with dogs, and the field is rich with diversity.

In spite of good intentions, these people may not have the same foundation for training and behavior work as one gets when they have gone through a certification program with a curriculum based on behavior theory, integrated these ideas by working with various dogs on different problems, and are required to maintain their certification with continuing education.

Behavior researchers have learned much in recent years. Good trainers use a variety of approaches, but all are based on an understanding of learning theory, specifically, operant and classical conditioning. This knowledge is then tailored to the personality of the individual dog, the specific problems and the goals of the handler.

Aren't There Just Good and Bad Dogs?
Do all dogs need to be trained? Don't you remember dogs who were perfect and didn't have any training? They were just "good dogs."

- Why are some dogs so good and others so "bad"?

- Won't my puppy grow out of her hyper behavior?

- If I start training too early, won't I break her spirit?

These questions are all valid. "Aren't there just good dogs and bad dogs," is a question that's often asked by owners who are puzzled by problems they are having. If the answer is yes, the temptation is to get rid of any dog who does not seem to naturally fit in with the family. If the answer is no, then the owner must decide whether he or she is willing to do what is necessary to help the dog become a good family member.

There is a small percentage of dogs who may be considered dangerous in the sense that no matter what you do, they will not fit easily into a family setting. This small percentage in no way matches the number of puppies and dogs who are abandoned or euthanized for behavior problems each year.

So why does this happen? The answer is that everyone has their own idea of what makes a good dog, and each different breed or mix has its own special talents. Some people want a dog to bark when someone comes onto their property, others don't like it when a dog barks. Some want a dog who is playful while others want a quiet, easygoing dog.

With the different wants of owners and the different traits and behaviors in different breeds, mixes or even different lines of purebred dogs, it is the unusual situation where the match between dog and owner is perfect. This is because many owners do not think about how the specific behavior of a breed or mix will fit in with their family. More often, a family will end up with a dog because the dog was inherited, he was taken in as a favor, he was a gift, he was cute or beautiful, he was small or large, he doesn't shed or he was like a dog they had as a kid. None of these situations guarantee a good match between owner and dog.

Because of the possibilities for a mismatch between a dog and a family, an owner may think his problem dog is bad or even aggressive. Research over the last decade or so shows that many of those bad behaviors occur because owners don't understand the ways a dog's behaviors are formed. Many owners are simply not aware of how to guide their dog to be the pet they want him to be. With training (of both owner and dog), unwanted behaviors can be prevented or changed in the vast majority of dogs. Even the dog who starts out as a mismatch can adjust and become a loved pet.

Basic Issues for Puppy and Dog Owners

Here is a list of issues that must be addressed early on or

they can cause problems later.

Veterinarian Relationship
Take your dog to the veterinarian within 48 hours after he arrives at your home.

- At that initial exam, discuss inoculation schedules, spay/neuter procedures, prevention of fleas and other external pests, prevention of heartworm and other internal worms, and exposure to dangerous diseases.

- Make a list of any questions you have and be sure to ask your veterinarian. Your veterinarian should be your first line of defense if a health problem arises.

- When a problem arises at home, most veterinarians are glad to answer some questions over the phone to determine if it is necessary to take your dog into the veterinarian's office.

Your dog should have a yearly veterinarian appointment for a check-up. **Remember, every year in a dog's life is roughly equivalent to seven years in a human's life.**

- That yearly veterinarian appointment is actually like checking a human every seven years.

- Some diseases can advance rapidly in a period equivalent to seven years.

- Your dog's annual check-up can help keep you ahead of some tough problems.

Identify the nearest veterinarian who offers emergency services, including night and weekend availability.

- When an emergency occurs, that is not the time to wonder what to do.
- Having a regular veterinarian for support and an emergency veterinarian when needed can make the difference between life and death for your dog.

- Best of all is when your regular veterinarian and your emergency veterinarian work together.

Dog License

Don't forget to check on when your pup must be licensed in your state or municipality. If your dog wears his tag on his collar, there is a better chance he will find his way home if he gets lost.

Purchase or Adoption Contract

Don't assume anything. Read the purchase or adoption contract and make sure you understand all of its provisions. For example, if your purchase contact says your pup will be replaced if he is diagnosed with severe hip dysplasia, via X-ray, on his second birthday, that is different than wording that says up to his second birthday.

Keep receipts and any documentation necessary to verify that you have done the things you agreed to do. If you have a problem, the contract could be all you have to fall back on.

Registration

If applicable, remember to send in your American Kennel Club (AKC), United Kennel Club (UKC) or other registration papers.

- There is a variety of registration organizations for all kinds of specialty animals.

- Some breeds have their own registration systems and their dogs are not registered with the more common national associations.

- Some of these smaller registries exist because of the desire to keep tighter control over breed standards or because a national organization does not yet recognize a breed for registration.

- Mixed-breeds can also be given a special registration designation so they can compete in trials and competitions. Each organization has its own requirements.

Identification

To increase the chances of recovering your dog if he gets lost, we recommend that you consider having your dog tattooed or microchipped. Check with your veterinarian about options.

- If you choose a microchip and your dog becomes lost, most shelters and veterinarians will check to see if he is chipped.

- If you opt for a collar tag, consider putting *family pet, reward and a phone number* on the tag. I was once told not to use the dog's name because it can help a would-be kidnapper make friends with the dog.

- On our tags, we put: *family pet, microchip, reward and two phone numbers,* ours and the one for the microchip company.

Rides in Cars

Some dogs love riding in the car and some become carsick. If you want your dog to be comfortable in the car, here's a good way to get started.

- Start with frequent, short rides the length of your driveway.

- Then drive around the block; then a little farther.

- Gradually increase the length of rides.

- Make the destination as positive as possible. So, for example, don't take the dog in the car only when it is time to go to the vet.

- Try feeding your dog in the car (while it's parked).

- Hide treats in the car so your dog regards it as a good place to be.

- If your dog continues to become ill when on rides, check with your veterinarian for medication options.

Grooming

Different breeds and different owners have their own personal requirements regarding grooming. Our adult dogs are bathed and have nails trimmed and ears cleaned every four to eight weeks, depending on the individual dog's needs. Nails must be checked more often than the bathing, although some dogs get pretty dirty very quickly. Brushing should be done as needed.

If you don't want to do these things yourself, shop around for a groomer who likes dogs and with whom you are comfortable.

- Some groomers operate like an assembly line with little consideration for the animal. Other groomers truly love dogs and it shows in the way they relate to the dogs during the grooming process.

- Groomer prices vary, which is another reason to shop around. But please don't choose solely on price.

- To prepare your dog for grooming, make it a point to massage all parts of your dog's body often. This helps the dog when he is handled by groomers and veterinarians.

- As you massage the dog, check for bugs, bumps and other potential problems.

An excellent groomer told me to make the whole grooming process predictable for the dog. That means do the same things in the same way using the same tools and the same words. If you take the dog to a groomer, try to use the same person every time. That will help the dog to be more comfortable. If you do the grooming yourself, use the same process every time.

It's much easier to work with a puppy than to wait until you have a high-energy adolescent who wants nothing to do with a bath. Do each of the stages suggested here on different days; don't jam it all into the day you want to give the first bath. If you are lucky, this kind of preparation can go a long way toward making the bath experience more relaxed.

- To make it easier, get the dog familiar with the grooming site using positive rewards.

- Take the dog to the tub room and give some treats.

- Put him in the tub and give some treats.

- Wet his feet and give some treats.

- Work your way up the dog with water slowly, especially if the dog is scared.

- As much as possible, connect treats with the process.

Chewing
All dogs chew. We think chewing is one way dogs deal

with anxiety. The trick is to give them things that are okay to chew. Do not give old shoes, gloves and things like that. Dogs can't tell the difference between an old shoe and a new one, so it's easier to just give them things that they can more easily identify as their toys.

- Although there is no such thing as a perfectly safe chew toy, we like nylon and rubber chew toys. They last a reasonable time and are made in different degrees of hardness, depending on how hard your dog chews.

- If you give your dog stuffed toys with squeakers, watch carefully because the squeakers could all end up in your dog's stomach.

- If you find your pup chewing on something you don't want him to, refocus him to something you approve of and that he also likes.

- If necessary, toss a treat to divert the dog while you pick up the undesirable chew object, then give the dog something you want him to have. Be sure to praise your dog when he takes your preferred chew.

- In tough cases, you might consider using a bitter-tasting spray or jelly on something you don't want the dog to chew; it usually deters them.

- Be cautious when using rawhide and other recently alive chew objects. Some dogs are more likely to become possessive of these chews.

When using rawhide and the like, I suggest doing it as a ritual. We give each dog a single roll rawhide (it holds up better) for 30 to 40 minutes each night. The dog is cued to sit, is given the roll and is then released. At the end of the allotted time, we remove the rawhide. In the early stages of teaching the dog this ritual, we tossed treats to distract the dog from the rawhide. Later, most dogs learn the process and relinquish the rawhide easily.

Dog Food

Dog food is big business. Don't be fooled by heartbreaking, cute or flashy advertising. Look at the ingredients. At the time of this writing, a moderate grade of dog food purchased in a large bag may cost about 50 cents per pound. A premium grade of food may cost $1 per pound or more in a large bag. Better food means you feed your dog less, so the expensive food is not really twice as expensive to feed. Less going in also means less coming out.

We are not nutrition experts, but we do have some experience with feeding dog food. Here is our best advice.

- When purchasing dog food, human grade ingredients are best.

- Meat should be listed first or second on the bag's ingredients list.

- Look for a superior protein source: meat or a single-source meat meal such as chicken rather than poultry meal.

- Avoid meat by-products and generically named fats or proteins, such as animal fat and poultry fat.

- Look for whole, unprocessed grains, vegetables and other whole foods, such as potatoes and carrots.

- Avoid food fragments such as brewers rice and corn gluten (although many foods contain one of these).

- Avoid sweeteners, including corn syrup, sucrose, ammoniated glycyrrhizin.

- Avoid propleneglycol, a moisturizer used in some foods.

The protein level of the food should also be considered. Unless you have a working dog, excess protein can give your dog excess energy that he must burn off. Without an opportunity for enough exercise, this excess energy can turn into annoying behavior in your home. We feed our non-working dogs food with protein levels below 25%—less in some cases, depending on the dog. Some people recommend protein levels between 18% and 22% for non-working adult dogs.

If you have questions about the proper protein level for your dog, consult your veterinarian or a nutrition specialist.

Rituals
Dogs respond well to regularly scheduled events. They will be easier to get along with if you set regular times for exercise, meals, bed, outside time, play and so on.

A Safe House

I seldom allow our dogs to run around in the house without supervision. They spend their time in the house with me or my wife. **After all, it is about the relationship.**

- With a new dog, it's important to baby-proof your house just as you would for a human baby.

- Don't leave a pup unsupervised and expect things to go well.

- You never know when your dog will catch the scent of a dead bug that was imbedded in the stuffing of your couch when the couch was manufactured. Once the scent is identified, if the dog is bored, digging into the couch is normal behavior.

- Dogs should show consistently reliable behavior over significant time (at least a month) before they are left alone unsupervised.

- Even then, the first times alone should be short to determine how the dog will handle this new-found freedom.

- Remember, if the dog can't show behavior you want when you are with him, it's a good bet that he will not do it when you are not present.

- To leave a pup or adolescent dog loose in a house or apartment while you are away is just asking for trouble. Consider using a tether, crate or safe room for the dog when you must be away.

The Crate

Think of a crate as a den for your dog. A den is a cozy place that the dog can seek when she wants privacy. It also serves you when you need a break or when you will be away. If introduced properly, the dog will feel comfortable in her crate.

To introduce the crate:

- Consider feeding your dog in the crate.

- Toss high-value treats in the crate and let the dog go in and out without closing the door.

- Hide treats in the crate for the dog to discover.

- After the dog willingly goes in and out of the crate, close the door for a few seconds, then reopen it.

- Move from a few seconds to a few minutes, then gradually to hours.

Crates help in housetraining. When used for housetraining, the crate should be big enough for the dog to stand up, turn around and lie down. If the crate is bigger than this, the dog may urinate or defecate in one part of the crate and move to the other end to sleep. That defeats the purpose of using a crate for housetraining. If your dog's crate is too big, consider putting in a partition.

Section 3. Common Concerns

Statistics suggest that only one-third of new puppies live their entire life in their first home. The other two-thirds are abandoned, left in shelters or given to others in the hope that the right home will cure their "problem." About 60% of the two-thirds that are given away are eventually euthanized. This adds up to millions of dogs being killed each year.

My Dog Has Issues

Many client calls are for help with an "issue." These issues can be rooted in digging, barking, scratching, nipping, separation anxiety, severe anxiety or aggression. Those who call want us to know that except for the issues in question, their dog is great. They also want to know whether we have worked with these problems before, is there hope, can this be cured and how long it will take to fix this.

These callers have expectations that range from realistic to out of touch. Expectations can often sound like this: "All I want is for my dog to stay on my property; come every time I call; sit and lie down when I tell him; stay until I say he can leave; protect my house and family; generally respect me as his master." All of these things are doable with the appropriate time commitment and expertise. None are doable in a six- to eight-week group class for around $80.

Some issues are more annoying than dangerous and can be resolved using simple management strategies. If you find that you have an issue I have not addressed, check the Internet. There are many organizations, such the Dumb Friends League of Denver, Colorado, as well as web sites maintained by private trainers, that have suggestions for dealing with specific behavior problems. When you're doing web research, you'll have to decide who to believe. Consider the material in this book that explains types of training and trainers. As you read this book, you may find that when you apply our foundation strategies and combine them with your own creativity, many of your problems are solvable at home.

My Dog Is Hyper

"Can you settle my dog down? He won't listen; he's just hyper!" These are among the comments we hear the most at our training center. The reality is that during adolescence, many dogs seem to have a never-ending supply of energy. If that energy is not channeled, it can be really annoying. I often tell clients that adolescence is the most difficult time in the dog owner's life. During this time, dogs test boundaries. This is the time when owners are looking for that benevolent farmer to provide acres of land so their dog can run free. If the owner does not have a management plan, many dogs are given away during adolescence.

Some hope that spaying or neutering the dog will get rid of this extra energy. Sorry, this is not as good a solution as some have been led to believe. One estimate is that you have a 50-50 chance to see a difference in energy level after neutering a male dog and probably no difference after spaying a female.

The best approach to deal with this high energy is to

develop a structure with definable, consistent boundaries. In addition, you must provide appropriate exercise, and you should have your dog on a training plan. If you do the things we suggest, your dog's hyperactivity and the annoying behaviors that go along with it can be managed.

Mental Health Issues

Serious issues that prompt an owner to contact their veterinarian or a training support system may be similar in nature to mental health issues in humans. The difference is that a human can seek counseling to discuss their problem. They can go through cognitive therapy, where they gain an understanding of what is happening. They can listen to explanations and reason through why their issue might be based in illogical assumptions. Yet, even with all this, many mental health issues humans face do not easily go away. Some people progress or resolve their issue with a combination of medication and therapy. Some remain in therapy and/or with the support of medication all of their lives.

To get a more personal feel for what these kinds of issues might be like for your dog, think about these examples.

- Are you be a person who is generally okay about life, except that when you are in heavy traffic or when your in-laws come to visit, you get anxious? This may be equivalent to a mild case of anxiety in a dog.

- Do you know someone who is very uncomfortable when he must balance his checkbook or go to a tax audit? That may be comparable to a moderate case of canine anxiety.

- How about the person who panics when they're even thinking about flying, or is incapacitated when speaking in public? Now you may be moving toward what it feels like for a dog who has a severe anxiety issue.

- Finally, what about the person who has so much rage that he or she becomes a spouse beater or bar fighter? Such a person just can't be in certain situations without blowing up. Here you may be seeing extreme anxiety or lack of self confidence— which can be at the root of very serious aggression in dogs.

Examples like these may help you better understand what it might like for your dog if she has a problem that is based on anxiety. Some humans do consider what the dog may be feeling; others are initially caught up in the worry, or fear of the consequences of the dog's problem. Even when humans do consider how difficult it can be for the dog, we can't talk to the dog to explain the issue as we see it. We can't get the dog's point of view and feelings. The only feedback we get is what we observe about the dog and how the dog reacts when we attempt to help.

When we work with a dog on an issue that has a mental health component, our approach is based on available research, our personal experience and the experience of others who have dealt with similar issues. Severe issues are always a challenge. There is no magic solution. Progress is about as easy to predict as it is for a person who is experiencing severe anxiety and is afraid to leave his home, or someone who thinks everyone is out to get her, or someone who has been mugged and insists on carrying a gun everywhere he goes. None of these problems are easily fixed.

For the human with these kinds of problems, their actions often seem perfectly logical to them. Likewise, for the dog, what we see as aberrant behavior makes perfect sense based on his experience of a particular environment, situation or the world in general.

For humans, we have counseling, support groups and in many cases medication to help us reach a point where such a person can function in society. For owners, veterinarians, trainers and behavior professionals who want to help dogs with these kinds of issues, we have behavior modification and also, sometimes, medication. But we are no more able to predict a timetable or a specific result than is possible with a human. So again, consider what it might really be like for your dog, be realistic, don't ask for a miracle, and if you get one, take it and be eternally thankful.

Separation Anxiety

Separation anxiety is an example of a mental health issue. This condition can be mild or it can be so severe that a dog may actually damage herself if left alone. Typically, a dog with separation anxiety will have an anxiety response within about 30 minutes after being left alone by her owner.

Common behaviors associated with separation anxiety include digging, chewing and scratching at doors or windows seemingly in an attempt to escape; and howling, barking and crying, possibly to call the owner home. Urination and defecation can occur, even with dogs who are housetrained. All of these behaviors can occur at an extreme level and can result not only in damage to the dog but dramatic destruction to the house. Floors may be torn up, walls broken through, curtains pulled down, furniture destroyed. All of this has happened to our clients.

All of this happens as the dog moves into a panic state as a result of the stress of being left alone. None of these things are done because the dog has been trying to "get even" or is "mad" because the owner has left her alone. It is strictly a result of a severe anxiety—a panic response.

A dog may experience separation anxiety under these circumstances:

- When a dog who is expecting constant human companionship is left alone.

- When a dog is left alone after being on vacation with the family.

- After the dog has spent time in a shelter or a boarding kennel.

- When there is a change in the family's routine or work schedule.

- When the family moves to a new home.

- In association with the addition or loss of a family member.

Because behaviors associated with separation anxiety can also occur for other reasons, it's important to verify that these behaviors are occurring when the dog is left alone. Dogs with separation anxiety tend to follow their owner from room to room, display frantic greetings and act excitedly when the owner prepares to leave.

If you suspect your dog has separation anxiety, call your dog's veterinarian, trainer or behavior professional to help you assess the situation and develop a plan to help the dog. Frequently, that plan involves the use of medication along with a carefully designed behavior modification program. Some people make the mistake of trying to cure the situation using medication only. The best results involve the use of both medication and behavior modification. Because you are dealing with a panic response, punishment is not an effective way to deal with separation anxiety.

Cases Examples: Separation Anxiety
The results of efforts to deal with separation anxiety vary. Three cases come to mind.

Case one: A dog was saved from death when he was adopted from a humane society. The dog destroyed thousands of dollars worth of curtains and furnishings while attempting to escape from his new home. He was an escape artist, but the owner would not give up. We worked with her for approximately a year. Medication was used. The vet and the dog's human companion worked hard to find the best medication and the correct dosage. The basic structure for establishing a relationship with your dog—as outlined in this book—was used as a foundation, and specific behavior modification plans were developed to fit the circumstances. The results were positive. The owner made some adjustments and the dog adapted. The owner should be rewarded in heaven.

Case two: The dog was adopted from a private shelter. The owner was not aware of the dog's separation anxiety. The dog had several panic attacks and urinated and smeared feces all over himself and his immediate living area. The owner worked conscientiously on this problem for several months, in conjunction with a veterinarian and with us. The dog made good progress. The dog was then left alone, had a setback, and was returned to the shelter, where the proprietor told the owner the dog would be cured by being kept in isolation until he got over it. These results were disappointing because we could see the dog was making progress but the owner just ran out of energy.

Case three: The dog was a purebred, purchased from a breeder. The owner was dedicated. The dog was put on medication for support and the owner diligently implemented the behavior plan we jointly developed. We communicated by e-mail every week. Within one month, the owner considered the dog to be almost perfect. These results are a good example of sudden (as opposed to gradual) progress—a miracle of sorts.

Nipping and Play Biting
Keep your fingers away from the dog's face and mouth. If new owners would do just this with puppies and young dogs, they would eliminate a big part of this problem.

Puppies and young dogs play using their teeth. Our job is to structure the play so they learn to keep teeth off skin and avoid nibbling on humans in ways that hurt.

Puppies learn some of this play structure from their littermates. They learn that when they bite too hard, they get a "yipe" response from their brothers and sisters. They learn that if they challenge mother, heaven forbid, there can be dire consequences. That's why it's important to keep puppies with their littermates for at least seven weeks, even if they are weaned.

Once the puppy joins our human family, we pick up the responsibility for teaching him. Some trainers promote the "yipe" method when a puppy bites. That means yipe like it hurts, even when it doesn't, and ignore the puppy for several minutes. Ignoring should be done as described in Section 13. Generally, it includes closing up your body, avoiding eye contact, keeping your appendages out of reach and not moving.

One key here is not to provoke behavior that results in nipping or biting. When it happens, ignore it. Wear appropriate clothes when you play with your dog so that while you are ignoring, the pup can't bite you. That means long pants and long-sleeve shirts—heavy clothing, if necessary.

Finally, keep your fingers away from the front of the dog's face and his mouth. If the dog bites, even a little nibble, stop interacting with him and either ignore him or move away from the dog. If he follows and nips, let him drag a house leash so you can control him. Try redirecting him to a chew toy or get him to play fetch. If these things don't work, put him in his crate or tether him until he settles down.

The Aggression Factor

For some dogs, their response to confusion or mixed messages from their owners or their environment may be seen as aggression. This "aggression" often proves scary to the dog's family. In many cases, an owner's response to this "aggression" is to confront or punish the dog. If the dog reacts to the owner's punishment, the next move may be to remove the dog from the home.

Often, confrontation may make the situation worse and removing the dog from the home may not be necessary. Some people think the best way to deal with this kind of problem is by having a trainer or a behavior professional have a "talk" with their dog—meaning "teach the dog a lesson." In our experience, that is not a valuable approach.

Each person with a perceived dog aggression problem also has an idea about what they hope the solution will be. When it's two dogs attacking each other, the desired solution may be that the two dogs get along again without supervision. Fortunately, many aggression-related issues can be resolved. Unfortunately, some can not be worked out in the way a client might imagine.

Some problems may only be resolved by the use of good management techniques. For people who live a busy life, work two jobs or have little children, management may not be desirable or realistic. For clients with these or similar lifestyle realities, serious soul searching is required. I'd rather see a dog be rehomed than take a chance on the safety of children or the infirmed in a home where management is not realistic.

Owner Fear

If you are afraid of your dog, your situation becomes more complex. Denying that you are afraid of your dog is even worse. Fear makes us do things we wouldn't otherwise do. If something your dog has done or is doing scares you, get help immediately. Discuss your concerns with a behavior professional or your veterinarian.

You always have options. The longer you let a difficult situation go unaddressed, the fewer options you may have. If your dog is acting aggressive, get help immediately. Once a dog bites, most rescue organizations are hesitant to help. If you have children or infirmed adults living with you and if your dog might bite, is large, and could cause serious damage, you may need to consider rehoming the dog. Discussing the situation with a professional may help you better sort things out and experience less guilt if the decision is to remove the dog from the home. My personal belief is that you don't take chances with children or elderly adults.

Multiple Dog Families

Having first lived with a loosely associated neighborhood dog pack, then with a single dog for 15 years, then with three, five and as many as 24 dogs (14 adults and 10 puppies) when I was active in breeding, I can testify that there are major differences as you increase the family dog population.

The multiple behaviors that must be dealt with as one adds a second, third or more dogs can be overwhelming. The problem is further magnified by inaccurate and inappropriately applied wolf research that suggests all wolves live in harmony under the supervision of a confident pack leader. Add in the belief that dogs are also pack animals, just like wolves. Then, presume that dogs should get along in any home pack environment we impose as long as there is an alpha (human or canine) to keep things under control. It's a recipe for some serious problems.

When I am contacted by someone who wants help with a multiple dog problem, I always take a deep breath and wonder how realistic the person's perspective will be. Sometimes the problem can be resolved, sometimes not in the way the owner thinks it should.

The best summary of this issue that I have seen is by Temple Grandin in chapter 2 of her book *Dogs Make Us Human* (2009). She gives an overview of research on wolf behavior, noting that wolves live in small, well-controlled packs of related individuals. They establish their own range and rarely welcome outsiders. When dogs were put into a simulated wolf pack situation, they did not operate in the same way.

Wolves learn both aggressive and submissive behaviors as they mature. Aggressive behaviors are learned first, so that cubs and adolescents are able to protect themselves if attacked. As wolves mature, they learn submissive behaviors that can be used to save their lives if they are confronted by a bigger, stronger wolf who could do them harm. With wolves, both aggressive and submissive behaviors are learned within a family relationship. These factors, combined with the freedom to establish their own pack, are what make it possible for the wolf pack to work.

This is not the way it is with dogs. Grandin reports that when dogs were put into simulated pack situations, things did not go well. It seems that the dogs had not developed the submissive behaviors needed to negotiate a family relationship with peers. This occurs because humans want their dogs to maintain a puppy-like demeanor throughout their lives. To achieve this, dogs have been selectively bred to maintain puppy-like behavior characteristics. Compared to wolves, dogs never grow up; they never mature in the sense that a wolf does. Because dogs remain puppy-like, they do not always develop submissive behaviors, as wolves do.

From Grandin's perspective, this all leads to the conclusion that "anyone who has more than two dogs better know what they are doing." Humans seem to want to put any assortment of dogs together in an imposed family structure, sometimes in very small spaces, and we figure the dogs should just get along. When you analyze it in a rational way, this just doesn't make sense.

Case Example: Father and Son

At a seminar where a well-known dog behavior specialist was speaking, a participant posed a problem that existed between a father and son in her kennel. It seems the father and son had clashed, possibly over a female in heat. The bad blood continued beyond the heat cycle of the female, with both males willing to fight at any time. The kennel owner was particularly distressed because during her many years of breeding, she had never had a dog fight problem.

The behavior expert told her she was lucky she'd never had a fight before and that it was likely she would have to deal with the two dogs using a management strategy. The kennel owner was relieved. I think it was because she believed she had to do something to get the two dogs to get along. Now she knew it just wasn't possible.

This is the reality for all of us who choose to have a multiple dog family. We can't count on the dogs to just get along. Putting two dogs together can be a crapshoot. Littermates can be even more of a crapshoot. Putting big dogs with tiny dogs is not only a crapshoot, it can be a death sentence for the smaller dog (if only by an accidental paw swipe to the spine). Even when two dogs get along for years, it's no guarantee that things will not change. A younger dog may all of the sudden decide she can take on the older dog. A push at the wrong time, when one dog doesn't feel well, can be the trigger.

The bottom line is, with multiple dogs you'd better know what you're doing. Don't be naive and put dogs in an imposed pack with no management plan and expect all to go well. Imposed packs need to be carefully built and managed. If they are not, in time the result can be heartbreak. Think carefully about how you will manage a multidog household. If you see a problem brewing, don't deny it, take action. If you need help, get it.

Siblings

Complicating the multidog family are sibling relationships.

Brothers and sisters add just one more dimension that must be dealt with. What often happens here is that a would-be pet owner goes to a breeder or rescue organization looking for a companion. On their search, they find the cutest dog… who has been kept with his brother or sister. What happens next is: "I couldn't bear to separate them," so both dogs go to the new home.

Now begins the saga. If siblings have been kept together, they can develop what I might call a dysfunctional relationship. This starts because they have likely been together since birth. If they're always kept together, they may not have developed independently. One may have counted on the other to do the exploring while he or she held back. In general, they may be more dependent on each other than is good when you are trying to make them a part of your family.

What sometimes seems true is that siblings spend time undoing the things that humans want to teach them so they can be good pets. To combat this, I recommend that owners consciously work to develop an individual relationship with each sibling. Be sure each dog gets individual play time and individual training time. Provide enough separation that each can develop an independent personality. Work through the structure suggested in this book with each dog. If you do these things, you have a good chance to head off potential problems.

Family Protection

Protection of the family is a hot topic. Most people hope that their dogs will protect them when the chips are down. Once they become attached to their family, many dogs are protective. That does not mean the dog understands what to do or when. Having a dog who is trained to protect requires intense work for both the dog and the handler. Not all dogs are up to the challenge and not all handlers are willing to commit the time needed to do the basic training and the continued workouts that are necessary to keep the dog sharp and clean. Even if all the protection training is done, one can never be sure if the dog will perform under pressure. Even some police dogs fail under pressure.

A sharp protection dog knows what to do when cued. A clean dog stops when told. A protection dog who is not sharp and clean is dangerous. He may not protect when needed, and if he is not clean, he may bite when not appropriate or not let go when cued. In any of these cases, the dog may be put to death and the owner may be sued.

For most people, the presence of a family dog who is well trained in obedience may make the most sense. Such a dog is a deterrent just by being there. Certain breeds, such as the German Shepherd, seem more naturally protective, a bit suspicious, and may be likely to ward off most unwanted intruders.

Good Obedience

Training a good obedience dog is a process. The breed you select, the methods you choose, the goals you have and the amount of time you are willing to commit ultimately determine the end result. Most breeds have been selectively bred to be able to perform specific jobs. If you get a Siberian Husky, you may have a natural sled puller and you will have a much bigger challenge if you want to train her to be a competitive obedience dog. Both can be done, but one will be easier than the other because of the nature of the breed.

Be realistic about what you expect. Dogs are living beings, not remote-controlled devices. Life with your dog should be about a relationship that is mutually satisfying.

Canine Intelligence

All of us, at one time or another, may wonder how smart our dog really is. Like parents, we want a bright child... I mean dog. And we want ours to be at the top of the class.

The intelligence of dogs has been written about and debated extensively. The problem with answering the question, "How intelligent is my dog?" is that each dog breed was developed for a particular purpose. When performing that purpose, members of that breed generally can't be beat.

Take the Bloodhound: no other breed can track like the Bloodhound. Or the Malamute: no other animal can move as much weight over as much territory on as little food, in a frozen environment than the Alaskan Malamute or his cousin the Inuit Dog. Or how about the Border Collie, often thought of as one of the smartest, at least where herding is concerned. And the various terriers: no dog is as fierce or clever in a face-off in a confined space as a terrier.

The bottom line is: intelligence is related to the circumstances the dog lives in and the genetic package the dog was born with. A great herding dog may be a very difficult pet to own if she gets no exercise and no opportunity to exercise her mind. When people ask about the intelligence of their dog, they are usually thinking in terms of compatibility in a pet home. In reality, not all dogs rank high on these criteria.

In fact, a dog rated to have low intelligence based on ideas of traditional obedience may be the smartest in her breed's specialty area. For example, a Malamute can make a great pet, but he is always a Malamute and he will always have Malamute traits. Malamutes are very bright dogs and yet they are not always considered the easiest dog to train as housepets. This does not make the Malamute a low-intelligence dog.

As a family pet, some breeds fit well if a person has done research—not just looked at pictures. When a dog is obtained based on a realistic understanding of the circumstances the dog will live in and the natural proclivities of the dog, the results are usually satisfactory. The results can be good to excellent if the human develops a clear structure and communication system with their canine companion.

Even a great dog is at a disadvantage when put into unrealistic circumstances. A common example is the large breed dog, perhaps a Labrador Retriever (known as a good-tempered breed) who is purchased as a puppy to be the companion for an older parent or grandparent. As the dog matures and reaches adolescence, the situation can become untenable. The dog becomes so physically strong and active that he makes life miserable for his owner. In some cases, the dog in this situation may be considered unintelligent because of his unsuitable circumstances.

Finally, no matter what the breed, **any individual dog can**

make a liar out of any generalization.

Developing a Relationship

To develop a great relationship, we must be aware of how we interact with our dogs 24 hours a day, not just when we want to give the dog a command to sit, lie down or behave. We need to be aware of the signals we send—both formal cues or commands (which we might use about 20% of the time), and in the ways we interact with our dogs informally (the other 80% of the time).

When you look at those numbers, you realize dogs are only on formal cue or command a small percentage of the time they spend with us. The rest of the time, they are expected to show the kind of manners that make our time together enjoyable. The problem here is that some people think dogs should automatically figure out what they ought to do to make us happy.

For the occasional wonder dog, this works. If you have owned one of these wonder dogs, it can make it all the more difficult to understand why it doesn't happen for all dogs. The fact is, if we don't make it a point to be clear with our dogs about all aspects of their life, they often get mixed messages about when it is okay to play, how rough to play, when to be a guard dog and when to relax and let your friends in the yard.

Owner education and good training can help manage the traits and personality of any breed. In the many cases where a dog has not been chosen to specifically match family circumstances, a lot can be accomplished with a clear structure, good training and understandable communication.

Section 4. Play and Exercise

Exercise: Can't Live Without It

Dogs must have exercise to be able to relax and function as good partners. Without exercise, excess energy and anxiety may contribute to destructive or other unwanted behavior. Exercise can consist of walking, jogging, play, sports, agility or herding.

Puppies need exercise, but they shouldn't be driven to exhaustion. As your puppy grows up, discuss the distance of his walks with your veterinarian. Puppies also should not jump where the landing will jar their soft bones and joints.

Adolescent dogs are at their physical peak. They need opportunities to get rid of their excess energy. If they don't get these opportunities, they may seem like a pestering menace, going from person to person jumping, pushing and bumping.

Adult dogs and senior dogs need age-appropriate exercise. Again, consult with your veterinarian at your dog's annual physical examination about the appropriate level of exercise.

Exercise needs may be different for different breeds. Dogs with brachycephalic (flattened muzzle) faces and dogs with heavy fur coats may need special consideration in warm weather. Dogs with short coats may need to wear a coat when they go out in very cold weather. Even within a breed, one particular line of dogs may need more exercise than another. This can make a difference in how well the dog fits into your household.

Generally, walking your dog is good exercise for both you and the dog. It helps solidify the bond between you. Turning your dog loose in the backyard or at a dog park may do little to encourage exercise. Active walking and playing moving games are not only good exercise, they challenge the dog mentally. A 20-minute walk away from your property each day stimulates both the physical and mental abilities of your dog.

Case Example: Dog Choice

If you are looking to buy a German Shepherd Dog, you may be impressed with a pup whose parents were imported from Germany. Later you may find that your pup came from working lines. Dogs from working lines may have been selectively bred to be very intense. This intensity may not make that pup easy to live with as a housepet.

If you are looking for a Labrador Retriever, lines that are bred for hunting are likely to be more high-energy than lines bred as pets. Good breeders will tell you the truth about their dogs. Those whose primary goal is to sell puppies may not. You need to be an educated buyer.

Treadmills

A treadmill is an acceptable form of canine exercise when it is used appropriately. We have helped clients teach their dog to walk on a treadmill. A special "dog treadmill" is not necessary; any type will do as long as the walking bed is long enough for the dog's stride and the motor and belt are smooth. As with humans, your dog should be evaluated by his doctor before starting on any strenuous exercise program. Various tips about treadmill operation are available from the suppliers.

Fetch

A game where your dog fetches an object and brings it back to you is good exercise. Some people modify the game so they can sit at the top of the stairs and toss a ball down the steps for their dog to fetch and bring back. In this kind of game, I like to use three cues: "Get It," "Take It" or "Fetch" is the signal to go out as I throw the object; "Bring It" is my encouragement for the dog to bring the object too me; "Drop It" is my signal to drop the object in my hand.

If the dog refuses to drop the object, I put my hand on the object and say "Drop It" again. If the dog pulls the object back in an attempt to play tug, I say "No" in a normal tone of voice and follow the dog's pull stroke (that is, I hold on but offer no resistance). At the end of the pull stroke, I again say "Drop It" (or whatever my chosen cue is). I continue to repeat this cycle while following the dog around, not allowing the dog to make a game from his pull stroke.

I continue this sequence until the dog realizes that pulling the object is not fun without my participation. The dog never gets to have fun with the pull stoke because I don't resist, I go with it. While doing this, I am sensitive to the dog's mouth pressure on the object. As I notice the pressure loosening, I take the ball and say "Good Boy" (telling him he did the right thing).

Once the object is relinquished, I often cue the dog to sit or do some other behavior. Then I throw the ball again as a reward for performing the requested behavior. Your go-out word ("Fetch") is a recognizable cue, so dog is allowed to get up from his sit to go after the object when he hears it. (We'll get to this later, but basically, the dog should end a behavior when you say it's okay to do so by giving him another cue.)

In play, one of the things I take into consideration is the length of time a dog wants to play the game. I am a big believer in quitting before the dog does. If the dog will fetch eight times, I quit at five or six. That keeps the dog wanting more in the future.

Rough Play

I recommend that humans play with their dog, not against their dog. When dog owners play rough, confront their dogs, push them away, bump them, hold them down, roll them around, lie on them and the like, they may be setting the dog up to make a mistake. By that I mean the dog is being led to believe it is okay to play rough, possibly put teeth on human body parts, growl, bark and lunge at humans. Allowing or encouraging these kinds of behaviors with even one person in the family may set the dog up to believe that it is okay to do those behaviors with anyone. In the wrong situation, this can cost the dog her life and the human a lot of money.

I suggest that rough play between a human and a dog should only be part of a specific activity, such as a working dog sport, where the necessary safety precautions are in place. Schutzhund is an example of a working dog sport. In

Schutzhund, dogs are taught to track, protect, attack on cue, escort a person in custody, conduct themselves with good manners and follow cues without hesitation.

The bottom line, in most cases, is that dogs are much tougher than humans in a pound–for-pound, one-on-one fight. That's why in sports like Schutzhund, the human in the struggle wears a heavy padded suit.

When a human involves himself in rough play with his dog, the dog is in a difficult situation. The dog has to figure out how rough she can get without going too far. Not a fair deal for the dog.

Playing Tug

A game of tug between a dog and a human has some controversial elements. Many trainers, usually those who are traditional in orientation, believe that tug brings out aggression in dogs because it encourages them to use their strength against a person. Other trainers, often more contemporary in orientation, don't believe that is necessarily true. There is also a difference of opinion about what a tug game is. One position is that it is a game that pits the owner against the dog. Another position is that the human and the dog are beating up the tug toy. So what does one do?

My position is this: if you want to play tug and if your dog has not shown any aggressive tendencies so far, you can play tug if you follow the rules below. If your dog begins to show any aggressive tendencies, the tug game should stop.

Rule one: The dog only plays tug with authorized

personnel. That means those who know the dog, understand the dog and are willing to play by the rules. I recommend keeping this number small, never including strangers, and usually not including children as authorized personnel.

Rule two: Use only one tug toy and always keep it hidden away between games. This rule, combined with rule one, helps keep the dog focused on the game. When you are ready to play tug, you and the dog go to the storage place and get the toy.

Rule three: You get the game going. As you play, you should win about half the time. If necessary, you can teach the dog an "Out" cue to let her know she should let go of the toy. **Teaching "Out"** involves signaling the dog with a verbal or other cue that she should release the toy. To do this, stop resisting the dog's tugging, show the dog a treat and say "Out." Usually, if the treat is of high value to the dog, she will release the tug toy and take the treat. You say "Good Girl" and then ask the dog to sit. If she sits, you say "Good Girl, Okay," and restart the tug game.

Rule four: On several occasions when you are in possession of the tug toy, you should ask the dog to do a simple task, such as sit. If the dog does sit, she is telling you two things. One is that she is not so agitated that she can't comply with your behavior cue. The other is she is willing to comply with your request. It the dog complies, you say "Good Girl, Okay," and restart the tug game. If the dog can not or will not comply with your simple cue, you say "Too Bad" and put the tug toy away. You can try again a few hours later or the next day.

Rule five: The dog's teeth must never touch your skin. If they do, you instantly say "Too Bad" and put the tug toy away. The phrase "Too Bad" is used as a marker to signal the dog that the associated behavior results in the end of the game.

Rule six: Don't leave the tug toy out when you are done with the game. Put it back in storage.

Rule seven: Don't play tug with any other toy.

These rules help prevent you from setting your dog up for a mistake.

Toys

Dog toys are everywhere. Stuffed toys, squeaker toys, you name it—stores will sell it if people will buy it. Because toys can vary so much in how safe they are, it is a buyer-beware world. Safety is a complex issue and partly depends on your dog's size, activity level and preferences. Another factor is the environment in which your dog spends time. Although no one can guarantee a dog's enthusiasm or safety with any specific toy, there are some guidelines. The following list includes suggestions from the Dumb Friends League of Denver, Colorado.

Be cautious. The things that are usually most attractive to dogs are often the very things that are most dangerous. Dog-proof your home by safely storing string, ribbon, rubber bands, children's toys, pantyhose and anything else that could be ingested. Avoid or alter any toys that aren't "dog proof" by removing ribbons, strings, eyes or other parts that could be chewed off and ingested. Discard toys that start to break into pieces or have pieces torn off. Chewies such as rawhides should only be played with under your supervision. Very hard rubber toys are safer and last longer. Take note of any toy that contains a squeaker. Squeaking objects should be used only under your supervision.

Toys should be appropriate for your dog's size. Balls and other toys that are too small can easily be swallowed or become lodged in your dog's throat. With small dogs, I'm always surprised at how big a toy they will play with. I have seen a four-pound dog wrestle a foot-long single rolled rawhide for an hour with complete satisfaction. As long as your dog is interested and the toy presents a challenge, it's probably not too big. Most small dogs don't seem to think of themselves as small. Do some testing with the size of toys your dog likes.

Toys are not a luxury, they're a necessity. Toys help fight boredom when dogs are left alone, and toys can even help prevent some problem behaviors from developing. Dogs are often willing to play with any object they can get their paws on. That means you'll need to be particularly careful about monitoring your dog.

Active toys made of very hard rubber, such as Nylabone-type products and Kong-type products, are available in a variety of shapes and sizes and are fun for chewing and for carrying around. Rope toys are usually available in a dog-bone shape with knotted ends. Tennis balls make great dog toys, but keep an eye out for any that are chewed through and discard them. Also notice if your dog's goal is strictly to destroy toys like a tennis ball. Toys that can be torn to pieces and swallowed can end up lodged in your dog's innards.

Distraction toys such as Kong-type toys and a variety made by Premier Products, especially when they are filled with treats or a mixture of broken-up treats and peanut butter or cheese, can keep a puppy or dog busy for hours. Only by chewing diligently can your dog get to the treats, and then only in small bits. We have also put kibble in the Kong, drizzled water over the kibble, added some cheese, put it in the freezer, and then given it to our dogs on hot days. Be sure to choose a toy that is the appropriate size for your dog.

Puzzle toys are very popular with trainers today. These toys are specifically designed to encourage a dog to use his problem-solving abilities to manipulate the toy and get the prize. They are great toys. We all know how smart our dogs can be. Thought-provoking toys help dogs build their mental abilities.

Soft stuffed toys are good for several purposes but aren't appropriate for all dogs. For some dogs, the stuffed toy should be small enough to carry around. For dogs who want to shake or "kill" the toy, the toy should be the size prey would be for that dog (mouse-size, rabbit size or duck-size).

Get the Most Out of Toys!
- Rotate your dog's toys weekly by making only a few toys available at a time. Keep a variety of types easily accessible. If your dog has a favorite, such as a soft "baby," you may want to leave it out all the time.

- Provide toys that offer variety—at least one toy to carry, one to "kill," one to roll and one to "baby."

- Hide-and-seek is a fun game for dogs. Found toys are often much more attractive than a toy that is introduced in an obvious way. Making an interactive game out of finding toys or treats is a good rainy-day activity for your dog.

Many of your dog's toys should be interactive. Interactive play is very important for your dog because he needs active "people time." Such play also enhances the bond between you and your pet.

- By focusing on a specific task—such as repeatedly returning a ball, Kong or Frisbee, or playing hide-and-seek with treats or toys—your dog can use up pent-up mental and physical energy in a limited amount of time and space.

- This greatly reduces stress due to confinement, isolation and boredom. For young, high-energy and untrained dogs, interactive play also offers an opportunity for socialization and helps them learn about appropriate and inappropriate behavior.

All in all, play is an important part of a dog's life. As thoughtful owners, it is our job to see that play is conducted and toys are used in ways that end up being positive for the dog. Without our help, dogs may get into all kinds of trouble with their selection of play activities and what they choose to put into their mouth—and eventually, into their stomach.

Section 5. Finding a Training Plan

Some dog owners believe that, if training is even necessary, the only option is to attend a training class consisting of six to eight group lessons. In those classes, a dog is taught obedience commands. For others, dog training is a series of classes at different levels. Each level is designed to teach more difficult concepts, leading to competition in shows or trials that showcase the dog's abilities. For most of us, dog training is a process through which we develop a satisfying relationship with a loved companion.

Over the past two decades, a great deal of research has been done that has influenced the methods trainers use. These new methods have had a profound impact on both training approaches and the environment in which training takes place. There is no longer just one method. There are a variety of approaches that enable trainers and behavior professionals to be more skillful in matching their strategies to the needs of the dog and the values of the owner.

The success of any training program depends on the amount of effort the owner is willing and able to put forth. Make no mistake, good behavior does not occur without effort, and changing the behavior of a problem dog requires even more effort.

The cost of training depends on how far you want to go. Typical options include a basic evaluation, participation in group classes, individual private lessons at a training center, a trainer coming to your home, or you can even send your dog away for in-kennel training. In this section, we'll discuss each of these options. At Signature K-9 Training and Behavior, if we don't offer the service you want, we will recommend an appropriate resource.

When to Begin Training

Generally speaking, puppies should not leave their litter until they are at least seven weeks old. Some people believe that puppies can leave the litter as soon as they are weaned from their mother. This is not good practice. More than once, I have suggested that a potential client return a four- or five-week-old puppy to his litter until he is seven weeks old. Puppies learn from their mother and from littermates. Puppies removed early may miss valuable developmental lessons that can result in behavior issues later. Although these problems may be dealt with, they can cause frustration that is easily prevented by keeping the puppy with his litter for the appropriate amount of time.

Once you take the puppy home, he should be sheltered for about two weeks before beginning training. If, during this period, the puppy becomes ill, it may mean that the illness started at the breeder's facility. If the puppy remains healthy during this period, you may be fairly sure that nothing has come home from the breeder with your puppy.

Between eight and ten weeks of age, while the immune system matures, puppies should be introduced to as many people as possible in the safety of their home. During this time, it may be a health risk to take puppies to public places, including pet supply stores, where they might contact other animals who are transporting disease or parasites. About ten weeks of age is a good time to begin training.

Between four and six months of age, as the young dog moves into adolescence, independence-seeking becomes a focus. This independent stage may last for a year or longer, depending on the size and breed of dog. Adolescence is a time when clear communication and training is a must to minimize frustration for both dog and human. The earlier this training starts, the better for both.

Puppy School

Most puppy classes include basic instruction, socialization activities and games to help develop agility and confidence. Check with your veterinarian about how old your pup should be before she meets other dogs at a puppy class. Usually, a 10- to 12-week-old puppy can go to class if she is up-to-date on her inoculations.

Group Classes

Group classes have been the most widely available. In a group class, you buy a package of six to eight sessions that are about 50 minutes each. In group sessions, help with individual problems and setting up the right structure for home is difficult because of time constraints. The advantage of group sessions is that a dog gets to experience learning in a dynamic social environment.

Instructors for these classes may come from several sources: professional trainers are those who train to earn a living, club trainers are those who train as a hobby, and there are other types of self-designated trainers. The credentials of trainers vary.

Signature K-9 offers several types and levels of small group classes, depending on the skill and interest of dog and handler. To ensure that the dog will benefit from a class and be safe in a group, we start by working with the dog individually. There may be from one to four or more individual private sessions, depending on the dog. Dogs with severe problems may require a number of individual sessions along with gradual introduction into a specialty group, such as a class for reactive dogs. From a specialty group, the dog may progress into more general obedience or agility groups.

Private Lessons

Private lessons offer an individualized approach. They are usually done with an individual owner, as a family or with one or two other people with similar goals. In private lessons, a dog's specific problems can be diagnosed and strategies can be designed to manage or alleviate them. During our private consultations, a structure for living in the human household is established.

Basic behavior commands or cues are put in place and owners and family members are taught how to train their dog, solve future problems and manage or prevent difficult situations. In this format, everything is done one-on-one. Each dog and handler is known by the trainer or behavior consultant.

Training in Your Home

If you are unable to leave your home due to illness or because you cannot travel, you may want to consider in-home training. Basically, you will be paying for private lessons plus a travel fee. Travel fees are usually based on how far the trainer will have to travel in miles, plus consideration for time the trainer spends on the road.

Although some believe that a dog with problems is best trained in the home, where the behavior is displayed, our experience is that training can also be effective when the dog is brought to our center to be assessed and receive his basic training, and his humans can set up a behavior modification plan. Then, when the dog goes back to the home and the problem comes up, the owner has a specific plan for what to do and has had practice using proper techniques.

In-Kennel Training

In-kennel training means your dog stays with a trainer for a period of time ranging from one or two weeks up to a few months. If you are interested in training with the least personal involvement, perhaps because you don't have the time, are unable to do the work, a special skill is needed or your dog has a serious problem, this type of training might be for you.

In this training format, the professional trainer works with your dog several times a day to teach a set of behaviors that have been specified in a contract. After the initial residential period, the trainer teaches the owner what the dog can do and how to keep the dog working at home. For this method to be successful, the owner must follow the instructions set out by the kennel trainer. If the owner does not follow through, the dog will lose her training.

The Most Important Consideration

When you're looking for a trainer, the most important things to consider are can you live with the methods used with your pet and can you feel comfortable with the individual you are working with? If the answer to either of these is no, you are likely to be uncomfortable about the way your dog is treated.

The best way to make decisions about a trainer is to read the written material they put out and talk with them either in person or by phone (e-mail may also work). Ask questions about the things that concern you and that will be factors in your comfort.

In the next section, you will find a discussion of traditional versus contemporary trainers. Trainers who fall into these categories use substantially different approaches. You should get to know all prospective trainers and explore their approach fully. When talking with trainers, any question is fair game as long as you are polite. If a prospective trainer or behavior consultant acts as if you should not be asking a particular question, that is reason for caution on your part.

Locating Trainers

To find lists of trainers in your area, the following web sites may be helpful. Each of these groups has a "trainer locator" on their web site. Just look for the locator and follow the directions to type in either a zip code or a postal address, and you will be given a list of trainers in your area.

- **Association of Pet Dog Trainers (www.apdt.com):** founded by Ian Dunbar, this organization is generally a contemporary, rewards-based training group

- **International Association of Canine Professionals (www.dogpro.org):** this organization has both traditional and contemporary trainers

- **International Association of Animal Behavior Consultants (www.iaabc.org):** this organization's membership has a contemporary orientation; members are behavior consultants

- **National K-9 Trainers (www.nk9dta.com):** this organization is basically traditional in its training orientation

Picking Your Training Team

When you're ready to start training, you need to pick a training team. I generally suggest that anyone who lives in your home, as well as anyone who comes to your home frequently, should be considered part of your training team. It's very important that you know who is and who is not part of that team. Here are two criteria those on your team must meet:

- **Members of your training team must be *willing* to do what you ask** when interacting with your dog. That means you have a responsibility to make sure they know the proper way to interact with your dog. Either you must teach them or you must include them in the training process with your trainer or behavior professional so they can learn first hand.

- **Members of your training team must be *capable* of doing what you ask** when interacting with your dog. This means physically and mentally capable. You could have a 90-year-old grandmother who is willing but not capable. You could have a 15-year-old grandchild who is capable but not willing. It is your responsibility to make this assessment.

The reason for these criteria is that if you are working hard to teach your dog a desired behavior and someone else allows the dog to practice an incompatible and undesired behavior, your efforts will be seriously hampered.

Case Example: Stop Jumping
If you are trying to teach your dog not to jump up, you want everyone the dog comes in contact with to practice interaction that will discourage jumping. If someone says, "It's okay, I like it when dogs jump up to greet me" and then allows the dog to jump on him, that person is working against you in your training program.

In dealing with those who won't do what you ask when interacting with your dog, you must take control of the situation and your dog so that the dog will not be allowed to practice behaviors you don't want. If necessary, you may have to keep the dog on leash or in a crate when the person enters your house so that you can control the dog's behavior.

Analyze Your Options
Analyze your situation and pick your team carefully. The right team can make training and living with your dog

much easier. If you can convince capable people to participate in your training plan and can teach them the behavior interactions you want, you won't have to work as hard and the dog will get the message more quickly.

The responsibility for assessing who is both capable and willing rests with the dog owner. If you have small children, they may not be willing or in some cases able to do what is necessary and safe to interact properly with your dog. You have to decide what they will be allowed and not allowed to do. You may also have to set ground rules with young children: "If you run and the dog chases you around the house, you will not be able to play with the dog." I know this might sound harsh, but it is inappropriate behavior on the part of children that can end in a nip or bite that is then interpreted as bad behavior on the dog's part.

Good old Uncle George may also be a problem. When Uncle George comes over, does he encourage your dog to jump on him or get on the furniture? If he does, and if those are behaviors you don't want, you've got to either teach Uncle George what to do or, if he is not willing to cooperate, be sure you are in control of the dog when your uncle comes to your house.

I know issues like this can be sensitive in settings with family and friends. Your job is to figure out how to pull it off without offending anyone. Remember, you can always blame it on your trainer... or the author of this book.

Supplements and Medication

Since I'm not a veterinarian, even writing generally about supplements and medication leaves me open to criticism.

Suffice it to say this topic will be considered in layman's terms. Your veterinarian should be your expert resource when dealing with supplements and medication. My purpose is to give a general overview of how supplements and medications may be used in conjunction with training and behavior work.

The term "supplement" can be used for anything from vitamins to calming tablets. Various powders, oils, pills and aromas are used to provide support for dogs. Brand names such as Rescue Remedy, Comfort Zone and DAP are examples of products that have been around long enough to be recognizable.

Dogs who have anxiety that may be contributing to behavior problems can often be helped with appropriate use of a supplement or medication. I often describe the options this way: A supplement or medication may be used to help take the edge off of the dog's anxiety. If a veterinarian has made the referral to us, he or she may already have prescribed a medication program to be used along with our behavior plan. If not, and if I sense that a supplement or medication might help the dog, I suggest that the client may want to consider using a DAP (dog-appeasing hormone) collar. A DAP collar looks like a flea collar but has an inert block attached that has a hormone imbedded. DAP is a manufactured hormone that creates an "all is well with the world" feeling in some dogs. The heat of the dog's body releases the hormone.

I see the DAP collar as an entry-level attempt to ease the dog's anxiety. We have had positive results with this device. DAP also comes in spray, atomizer and wipes. I like the collar because it is always with the dog. The collar lasts about 30 days.

Another old stand-by for dog owners is Rescue Remedy, a homeopathic mixture that is given to the dog in water or directly by mouth. It is administered in minute amounts. It is intended to calm the dog. Likewise, scents such as lavender are sometimes used to help relax the dog. There are those in the healing community who specialize in these kinds of supportive supplements. There are nutritionists, herbalists and even specialists and holistic veterinarians to advise you about the use of supplements and other alternative remedies. These resources were not available just a few years ago.

Veterinarians may prescribe tranquilizers or anti-anxiety drugs if deemed appropriate. Tranquilizers are sometimes used for short-term support. Anti-anxiety drugs may be used more long-term. Within these options, there are brands of medication that have been specifically formulated for and tested on dogs and there are those that are manufactured for humans. In some situations, veterinarians may prescribe for your dog a drug made for humans.

If your dog is put on tranquilizers, you may notice the effects. The dog may even seem a little tired or sluggish. If he's on anti-anxiety medications, you may not notice anything overt other than the fact that your dog may be a little less edgy. Tranquilizers may take effect very quickly, while anti-anxiety medications such as fluoxetine (Prozac) and clomipramine (Clomicalm) may take a few weeks to make a difference.

With any drug, there is a potential for side effects. Determining the appropriate dosage may take time and may require several contacts with your veterinarian. You may be asked to give updates on your dog so the veterinarian can adjust the dosage of the medication. In some situations, it may take some trial and error for the veterinarian to find the right medication and the correct dosage for your dog. Occasionally, it is not possible to find a helpful medication.

The current thinking is to use medication in combination with training and behavior work for difficult cases. For some owners, the idea of their dog being put on drugs is uncomfortable. My perspective is to try and look at it from the dog's standpoint. It is the dog, not the owner, who has the anxiety and in fact may be suffering every day as a result. When an owner arbitrarily rules out the use of medication, it is usually done without consideration of what it may mean for the dog.

Section 6. Assessing What's Real

The Map Is Not the Territory

With some preliminaries under our belt, we move to a more in-depth look at dog training and behavior management. To start, I use the metaphor, "The map is not the territory." What this means is that it is can be difficult to get the full meaning of something by reading or even hearing about it. It's easy to jump to conclusions, especially because we each have our own beliefs and biases. These pre-set ideas can trigger us to interpret something in a different way than it was intended.

This may happen to you when you read this book. I've personally experienced this over the years as I studied and observed trainers and behavior professionals. Often, they present two different personas. You see one when you read things they've written or hear them talk about their work; you see the other when you watch them work. When reading or listening, things may seem cut and dried— simple steps that will solve any problem imaginable. When you're observing the actual work, though, it soon becomes clear that what may start out as a clear path takes various turns, based on the dog's responses.

It's like when you read a road map: it doesn't give you a clear picture of how many switchbacks or giant potholes you will encounter if you leave the freeway to take a shortcut. It's also similar to when you look at a beautifully prepared menu in a restaurant; the pictures don't always give you an accurate idea of how the food will actually look—or taste. On the menu the images are often rich and luscious, while the actual food may be bland and tasteless.

As it relates to dog training and behavior, this can mean that what appears to be a simple set of guidelines can actually become very complicated, and applying those ideas to real dogs may not be so smooth... perhaps because the dogs have not read the book. It's not at all unusual for a potential client to call me and, while explaining his circumstances, tell me that he has purchased books or tapes but, when putting the principles to work, it did not go as represented in the manual.

My reason for bringing this up is that you may encounter the very same thing as you read this. You will tend to form opinions about me and about my methods, in part based on what I write and in part based on the personal biases and the expectations you bring with you as you read.

Each of us has a personal belief system that has been formed by what we have heard, seen and talked about over the years. We are especially affected by what we have heard from those we like and respect, such as our parents, friends, mentors and sometimes even television stars. We make decisions based on those experiences, sometimes without even being aware of how our beliefs have been formed.

To combat these phenomena, I have gone to great lengths to be detailed in my explanations. I have also stated on several occasions that if the things I suggest do not seem to work for you, please get help from a certified trainer or behavior expert. If things are not working, there is a possibility that you may be misinterpreting my writing or that your personal bias is pushing you in a different direction than I intended. It is also possible that your dog requires additional support beyond what I can put in this book. In any case, don't despair; just get help from a qualified source. And don't be surprised if the help you seek does not do things exactly the way I might. As I noted earlier, there are a lot of paths to the same solution.

Case Example: "No"

To illustrate how easy it is to be influenced, I went to a two-day seminar presented by a well-known author and trainer. The seminar was an extension of material the trainer had included in a book I often recommended to clients with fearful dogs. Overall, I was pleased with the time I spent.

So, what's the point? At the end of the seminar, the presenter decided to deal with the dreaded word No as it might be used in training or behavior work. I sat in the audience for 30 to 40 minutes while a rationale was presented for never using the word No. The short story is that this position was based on the idea that our human subconscious mind could not relate to a negative concept.

Did you get it? Even if the word No, as a concept, could not be handled by the human subconscious, we were not talking about humans. We were talking about **dogs**. Dogs don't come equipped with English, even as a second language. In fact, as far as a dog is concerned, what we call language is just a series of sounds—sounds that have no meaning until the dog learns a meaning that we teach.

The dog has no preconceived conscious or subconscious ideas about No. The dog only learns what the sound No means based on the association we create for the dog. If we associate the word No with intimidating body language or slapping a newspaper over his nose, the dog learns that No is something to be concerned about. **If the dog learns that No is simply a behavior marker that means "that's not what I want," it does not have any particular negative connotation.** So I spent 30 to 40 minutes listening to a discussion about the word No that had zero application to the world of dogs.

The bottom line is how easy it is to decide something is an absolute—absolutely right or absolutely wrong—with little information, erroneous information or misinterpreted information. This is of concern because those we look to for expertise can be guilty of expressing ideas that are not valid, yet those listening may give them credence because of who is presenting them. Be a cautious consumer.

Why You Should Care
You should care because any time you read, hear or observe what another person does, you should hold open the possibility that there is more to the story. This is particularly true with regard to dog training and behavior work. Whether it's your first dog or you have had dogs your whole life, the decision about how you will train is, or should be, one of your biggest.

Today there are options. Yesterday, there was pretty much one way: tell the dog what to do and punish the dog if he or she didn't comply. Today, you can choose more precisely how you want your companion treated during the training process.

In the world of dog training, I see two major differences in approach. One I categorize as "traditional training." This approach has been around for more than 100 years. The other I categorize as "contemporary training." Contemporary training has been around for several decades and is based on a conscious use of the available research into animal behavior.

Traditional Training

The fundamental premise of this approach is... pay close attention. The dog is safe when he is doing what has been cued or commanded by the handler. Yes, in traditional training the dog is told "Good Boy" when he does it right. But the big clincher is that the dog is punished when he doesn't get it right.

This punishment can be anything from a word, a swat, a collar correction (meaning a jerk that may be just annoying or one that literally shakes the dog's bones), to electric shock that may be applied at the neck, groin or any combination of other locations on the body. A typical tool of the traditional trainer is the "choke" or "slip" collar.

Did I get you? Did you rush to judgment based on the sound of what you are reading, or did you stop and ask yourself, Does everyone who uses a slip collar also use traditional training techniques? This is an example of how easy it can be to be triggered to jump to conclusions.

Contemporary Training

Trainers and behavior professionals whom I categorize this way are attempting to use more up-to-date information gleaned from animal behavior research. It's almost as if we've just awakened to realize that animal behavior research has been around for years—often as a basis for making decisions about humans—and maybe we should use it as we work with animals.

If you look at animal behavior research, it soon becomes clear that positive motivation makes much more sense and has fewer down sides than punishment. This is not to say that punishment does not work, especially when done by a well-trained handler. What it does mean is that if done incorrectly, with poor timing, too harsh or not harsh enough, it has a big potential down side.

By contrast, positive motivation, in the conventional sense, can get you to the same place with less down side and while developing a different kind of relationship with your dog. For me, the bottom line is: why would you use punishment on your loyal companion if there are other ways?

Case Example: 4-H

I once worked with a 4-H member who was doing the initial training of a dog who would eventually become as a service dog. The 4-H'er had done this before and had a plan about how to proceed. I came into the picture because the organization that would eventually train the dog wanted the dog to have some formal obedience training.

What I noticed immediately was that when this young

handler gave a cue to the dog, the dog would wince, back up, duck or shy away. It became clear that the dog was expecting to be "corrected" if he didn't do as ordered. This was the training method taught to the young handler in 4-H Club.

When I asked the trainer why the dog reacted this way, the response was one of confusion. When I suggested that the dog was worried about being punished, there was more confusion. The befuddlement declined as we worked with the dog using rewards when cues were completed.

This example points out the transition stage that dog training is in. Many people are still working as if their dog is a thing that should operate on a remote control rather than a living being who deserves respect and dignity.

The Extremes

Being what some would call a crossover trainer (meaning I started training in the 1950s when the traditional approach was pretty much it), I am well aware of the extremes that can exist in either of these training approaches.

The extreme traditional trainer will use almost any level of force to get compliance from the dog—anything, including correcting with a choke chain collar, shocking various parts of the body, pinning the dog to the ground, swatting the dog with various implements, even swinging the dog in circles off the ground to subdue him. Sounds pretty horrible, doesn't it? Remember, this is the *extreme* traditional trainer.

The extreme contemporary trainer may believe a dog

should never experience stress of any kind. At this extreme, some contemporary trainers might even allow a dog to be put down rather than use methods that would be considered aversive (involving discomfort) as part of a behavior modification plan.

Your Choice

As you pick a dog trainer or adopt a particular method to use with your companion, be sure you know what you are in for. In a book, you can check the table of contents or read ahead. When picking a live trainer, you need to know the reputation of the trainer and ask enough questions so that you feel comfortable. If a trainer seems defensive about your questions regarding technique, a red flag should go up.

Bias Influences Choice

Everyone has a bias about how things should be done. Mine is that animals are living beings and deserve to be treated with respect and dignity. At the same time, it seems unrealistic to me that any animal can live with no stress in his or her life. Consider your own life: is every day a bundle of joy? Do you never wonder or worry about what is coming next? Are you never startled, never concerned, never afraid?

If you are like me, you experience all these things. And if you are like me, what you hope is that you will be able to handle them and keep functioning in ways that guarantee your success and satisfaction. Likewise, I work with dogs knowing that some stress is bound to come into their lives. In fact, if there is no stress, I wonder if anything would seem reinforcing to them.

Case Example: Dysfunction

Some people feed their dogs homemade meals made up of roast beef, veggies and the like. They respond to their dog's every whim, often because the dog is in a constant state of whining, leaning on the owner, pushing with her head, pawing or barking demandingly.

They are literally feeding their dog to death and creating an environment where there are no expectations placed on the dog in exchange for the relationship with the human. Then, when the situation becomes intolerable, help is sought—perhaps because the dog has bitten and the owner realizes the dog could be taken away, perhaps because the dog will not get off the bed, will not come when called, refuses to walk on a leash, goes potty in the house... the list goes on.

When help is finally sought, the problem is complicated by the fact that the dog has experienced few expectations regarding his behavior and the owner would like the problem solved, sometimes without any changes in the dog's life. More to the point, he doesn't want to ask the dog to comply with anything in order to live in partnership with a human, yet behavior changes are desired.

The owner may tell me that the dog is not food motivated or will not work for food. In some of these cases, just one look at the plumpkin in question and you know why. The reality for me is that I have never found a dog who is not food motivated if the conditions are right.

Examine Your Bias

Look deep into your own biases. Be sure you know the

basis for your choices. Then pick trainers and methods that fit your needs.

Section 7. Know Thyself

It may seem odd to include a section about humans in a book about working with dogs. But when you think about it, humans are always at least 50% of the problem or 50% of the solution in any canine-human relationship. For that reason, leaving out consideration of what drives humans would leave a big hole in the puzzle we are putting together.

It's tricky to break down the components that drive humans. To do this in a practical manner, I've chosen a two-fold approach. The first element, our style, can be seen through observable behavior. The second element is what goes on inside our heads as judgments are made about everything in life. While style can be readily observed, the belief system that is used to make judgments is more elusive.

When working with dogs or people, things always go better if we first know ourselves. We need to understand what kind of behavior we use most frequently and what kind of impact our behavior has in various situations. And for a trainer or behavior consultant, it also means knowing enough about how style works so that we can identify the basic style of others. Understanding both self and others enables us to make conscious choices as we interact.

The second element to consider has to do with our thinking system. It can't be seen and isn't known unless it is shared or identified as we make decisions. It is the part of us that forms the belief system that acts as a filter through which we view the world. This filter sets the appropriateness standard as we evaluate everything we see, hear, feel and do.

It is the combination of our style and our belief system that determines how we operate with others and with our companion animals. It is this combination of factors and how we manage them that determines our effectiveness in all relationships.

Identifying Our Own Style

There are a number of ways to think about operating style. Some call it a profile, others think of it as personality or behavior tendencies. These are descriptions of something, but it's actually more important to understand what they are describing. That is, what is of most importance is that we know something about how we come across and why we react the way we do, particularly under pressure and unconsciously. This gives us insight about why things sometimes go well and sometimes not so well when we are working with our dogs.

As noted, there are two pieces to the style puzzle. The first is personal awareness. Are we a high-key Demanding Don, a light-hearted Social Sally, a laid-back Steady Eddy or a carefully controlled Analytical Alice?

We may all possess a little of each of these tendencies, yet it's common to prefer one or perhaps two of these styles over the others. This is not a conscious preference. Rather, it's something that we do naturally and without thinking.

Each of these general style preferences has inherent comfortable and uncomfortable ways of operating. Once we understand what our natural and most comfortable operating approach is all about, it's important to step back and look at how our approach works as we interact with our dogs and with others.

Style Descriptions

So here goes: I'm going to review four general categories to help explain operating style.

In Charge

Those with a take-charge style do not like leaving anything to chance. They may also have feelings of conflict about others who like to be in charge. Those with this style are outgoing go-getters. They jump right in, take chances and assess the results later. They may be among the first to become up-tight with their dog if she appears to be defiant or not willing to do what she is told.

Social

A person with a social-oriented style is outgoing and wants to have a good time. For this person, having fun is a criterion for success. If a situation seems tense or the dog seems to be unhappy, a person with this style is likely to be uncomfortable and dissatisfied. If a relationship is not attended to, they may become discouraged and not want to go on.

Steady

Those with a steady style are laid-back and level-headed. They want everyone to get along. They don't like situations where conflict is present and will try to negotiate consensus. Those with a steady style may be concerned about pushing their dogs too severely. The relationship with their dog will be paramount. A sense of team is the preferred atmosphere.

Analytical

Analytical people like details. They want to know the research and understand where opinions come from. They want to know why things happen. What makes the dog do this or that? Why won't the dog cooperate? Sometimes, psychoanalysis of the dog seems more important than solving the presenting problem. Not knowing the answers can cause this person much frustration.

These descriptions may help you get a handle on your own style. This awareness can help you be on guard and modify your style inclination to better relate to your dog as well as accomplish your goals.

For instance, if you know you get frustrated when you're not in control, you can intentionally work to remain relaxed and take a break if things get too tense. If you are more social or steady, you can convince yourself to hang in a little longer when you might otherwise want to quit. If you are analytical, you might allow yourself to trust a trainer with a good reputation to know what to do without giving you the minute details every moment.

A Best Style

I am not suggesting that there is a best style. Instead, we need to recognize the strengths in our style as well as where a given style might make us vulnerable in some situations. This understanding enables us to consciously manage and enhance our potential for success.

Getting It Done vs. Feeling Good

In stressful situations there must be a balance between accomplishing a task and not ruining relationships. If you have a hard-driving personality style, your tendency may be to push your dog harder when things are not going well. If you have a steady, easygoing style, you may tend to back off every time things get the slightest bit confusing or frustrating for you or for your dog.

If you favor a more social style, you may be so interested in having fun that you can't go on if any stress exists. If you are more analytical, you may have so many questions about "why" that you never get to working on the behavior at hand.

A more desirable outcome is possible when we are committed to accomplishing the task while also being aware of the part our unconscious operating style plays in the process. It is this awareness that can make the difference.

Style, Comfort and Competence

Style also affects success when it is related to our sense of comfort, particularly in new situations. We often feel uncomfortable in new situations or when we are learning something new. It's then that we may begin to doubt our competence. If we equate discomfort with the idea that we may not be competent, we limit our success.

If our most comfortable operating style tends to be structure and detail oriented, we will probably feel most at ease in situations where we are operating in a highly organized setting with clear, step-by-step directions. Not only might we want a detailed explanation, we might want to see pictures of each step and then a live demonstration. We may not care about humor or charisma, and we might hate it if someone takes what appears to be a very loosely structured approach.

Along with awareness that style is strongly connected to our comfort zone, it is also important to realize that we are capable of adapting our style to fulfill most tasks and relationship needs. We only need to modify our style, based on the situation, to enhance success. And, when doing so, remember that discomfort has nothing to do with our competence.

To maximize our style, we must become aware of the circumstances that make us uncomfortable. We must understand that each person's style brings with it some natural strength and some vulnerability. Strength can then be maximized and we can offset vulnerability by conscious personal choice.

What Dogs Want

According to one of today's top behaviorists, your dog may very well prefer you to have a personality style like Gandhi. My interpretation of that style is:

- Someone who can maintain their composure no matter what; a person who doesn't show frustration or anger to the dog.

- A person who knows when to get excited, when to remain calm and when to take a break.

- Someone who is clear and consistent about structure and guidelines.

- A person who can manage her style rather than let it manage her.

Section 8. Our Inner Voice

Our belief system and our personal values direct us in our thinking about our dogs, how they should be treated, what we should expect from them and how they should be trained. To become a good handler, owner or trainer, it's important to know how your belief system affects your actions. It's also important to realize that beliefs have only the validity that we personally assign to them.

The Voice That Haunts Us

The data that forms the basis of our belief system is composed of information collected through our life experience and stored within our memory mechanism. This collection of information is what directs the little voice deep inside us as we decide the way things should be.

Sometimes, that little voice is whispering so softly that we don't even realize it's present. Other times, such as when we back our car into a light pole, it screams at us with its opinions about how dumb we are or what a stupid place that was to put a light pole.

Many of us are so unaware of this little voice that when the idea is first introduced, we deny its existence. With further examination, we may find that it is this very same little voice telling us that no such voice exists.

The question is, Are we willing to consider that there is some mechanism, sometimes subtle and sometimes screaming, that informs our attempts to judge what is right or wrong? If so, then it is important to consider the origin and validity of information being used by that inner voice as it functions as judge and jury in our life.

A Computer-Based Analogy

To talk about our thinking processes in an understandable way, it's helpful to use a model or reference system. In his books *What to Say When You Talk to Yourself* and *The Self Talk Solution*, Shad Helmstetter develops a model that suggests our brain operates much like a personal computer. According to the model, programming takes place through sensory inputs such as sight, hearing, feeling and later by repetition of our own thoughts.

If you combine this idea with those of Morris Massey, author of *The People Puzzle*, it is possible to consider how our thought processes are affected by the generational influences we experience, particularly during our formative years.

We start with the premise that when we enter this world, much of the storage space in our personal computer has not yet been programmed. Since we know that there has been a continuing debate about the interaction of heredity and environment, it seems acceptable to consider that some of the storage space in our personal computer may have already been programmed at birth. Even so, there is still a vast amount of space available for the programming that takes place as a result of environmental influences.

Our first programming comes from our parents or those we live with at the start of life. To further the computer analogy, our storage files are continuously programmed by those with whom we come into contact as we move toward young adulthood. There is a recognizable logic to the way this happens. In addition to the influence of our parents, we may have close contact with extended family and friends of the family. What we see, hear and feel from those people adds to our files. In addition to people, the media that is available to us has a strong impact. Today, media is a formidable force. In past generations, it was less powerful.

As we move along in life, combinations of input from all aspects of our lives, especially those involving people who are significant to us, expand our files. What we see, what we are told and how we feel as we interact with significant others (be they boyfriends, girlfriends, a role model we admire or a person we detest) become part of our programming. At first, we accept this input without question. Later, when we are old enough to think through the merits of the input we have been exposed to, we can evaluate what makes sense and what does not.

Growing Up
With a basic understanding of this kind of programming, it is valuable to think about the nature of the information that comes to us through the process. Massey suggests that much of the information we take in is specifically related to the generation in which we grow up. During this time, we are bombarded with the political, social, family and personal issues of that generation.

In earlier generations, dogs were more likely to be outside pets with a job. On farms, the dogs ate scraps, protected the family and herded livestock. If they chased or killed chickens, they might be shot. In those times, dogs were more likely to be thought of as possessions than as unique beings, perhaps with rights.

In contrast, later generations with more disposable income may have developed a greater interest in more material possessions, including fancier pets. In these later generations, more dogs live in the home and many dogs have no particular job.

I was introduced to dogs by my grandmother and her dog Skippy, a Fox Terrier. After Skippy came another of my grandma's little dogs, Greta. Both were house dogs. My grandmother coached me on how to treat dogs and to watch out for Skippy because sometimes he got a little grumpy.

But for me, the formative years included a model where dogs were not generally allowed in the house. We had a neighborhood dog pack. The neighborhood kids each had a dog, even if this was not officially sanctioned by their parents. We had a Chow Chow, a Fox Terrier, a Cocker Spaniel, a retriever and a shepherd in our pack.

Everywhere the kids went, the dog pack went. We all contributed food and the dogs also scavenged for food on their own. Our parents just didn't want dogs in the house. As time passed, some of the neighborhood dog pack were killed on the road, some disappeared, one died from disease.

Good vet care was not considered important. Keeping dogs on leash or in kennels was also not important. All of these experiences contributed to my personal understanding of dogs and the circumstances they live in. It was only after making a contract to improve my high school grades that I ended up with a dog who officially lived with my family for many years.

In earlier generations, the message was that Mom should stay home and hold the family together while Dad went out to be the breadwinner. In dog training, it was mostly men at the helm and the usual approach was one of confrontation. Today, the message seems to be that both Mom and Dad can, and possibly should, be in the job market either to be sure the family has everything it wants or to provide personal satisfaction and fulfillment.

In the past, the message was that there were a limited number of professions appropriate for women. Today the message is that women can enter any profession they choose. And, if you'll notice, at dog behavior seminars women almost always outnumber men and the favored approach is to use positive motivation.

Evaluating Our Programming

It is important for each of us to take a look at what our life experience has provided and recognize that this program is now acting as a filter through which we view all reality and make judgments about everyone and everything—including how our dogs live and how they should be trained and cared for.

This process of evaluating everything through our own programming is always with us. This programming can be so complete that it is easy to assume that whatever it is that "I" think should also be the viewpoint of others. The problem with our life file is that when it was programmed, if we could have looked closely, there may have been questions about its accuracy.

Consider the trainer who learned his trade in the 1960s, when confrontation and punishment were considered the most appropriate way to teach a dog. If that person did not keep up with research and new ideas, he may continue to use methods that are now seen as less desirable and less effective. And it is likely that he will be willing to argue his point even in the face of heated opposition.

What's important here is that we become conscious of the information and ideas that are being used as reference points or "truths" when we make decisions. It is a difficult job to suspend the judgment that quickly comes to mind because of the experiences we have had. Yet, it is a necessity that we hold off those judgments until we have heard the viewpoints of others and collected current information that can be used to support effective choices.

In dog training and behavior work, this shows up as we assess problems, devise training plans and apply what is currently available through research. In this effort, research is thin because studies are expensive. Working with minimum research and a lot of opinion puts dog trainers and behavior professionals in a position to disagree.

Case Example: Beliefs About Training

In one discussion among professional trainers, the topic centered on the use of traditional training methods versus more contemporary methods—primarily, the use of punishment versus positive approaches. One comment directed toward a traditional trainer who had switched to a more positive approach went something like this: "Didn't you sense there was something wrong when you were using punishment?"

This is a perfect example of the way our programming works. When you are programmed to believe that a given approach makes sense, it is difficult to even conceive of another way. In this conversation, early programming affected both people. The formerly traditional trainer had been programmed to think that punishment was the appropriate way to operate. Until she was presented with a substantial body of information to the contrary, she never doubted her position. Here, the formerly traditional trainer is to be commended for remaining open to changes in research results and informed opinion.

With regard to the contemporary trainer who asked the question, her programming was so complete that she could not image how the formerly traditional trainer could have accepted her original paradigm. This kind of blindness can show up even in scientific research. A researcher with a strong bias toward a particular outcome can be blind to hard evidence that is contrary to that bias. It is this kind of paradigm blindness that locks our mindset so we may not even consider the views or the science of others.

Take operant conditioning, a model that includes a series of scientific terms used to tie behavior to consequences. The terms used are Positive Reinforcement, Positive Punishment, Negative Reinforcement and Negative Punishment. Although the model is founded in science and the terms are scientific in nature, some trainers and behavior professionals will not consider using punishment, while others are open to all options under appropriate circumstances.

To illustrate how difficult it can be to find consensus, think about what you believe about dogs thinking, dogs having emotions or dogs having a sophisticated two-way communication system. The science is thin on these topics, yet many of us have opinions. Our challenge is to remain open to what is yet to come.

Just the Facts, Please

Many of our decisions appear to be based on facts. But in reality, a large number of those decisions are not based on scientific facts but represent collected opinions, ideas and belief systems. Because of this, those with the most support can win the day and force a direction which, although popular, may not be the best decision available.

Dealing with deeply held views requires an understanding of their origin in us and in others. To have a chance for success, we must be conscious of the basis upon which we make decisions. We must acknowledge the beliefs we hold, then suspend judgment while we listen.

As we work with our canine companions, we must consider all points of view and seek out the sources of those viewpoints before we act. Finally, we must guard against the temptation to believe that we have been endowed with supreme intelligence, which funnels information to us that is irrefutable. In my work, this shows up in the intentional and careful use of statements such as "our current belief is" and "research seems to suggest" and even "my hunch or personal belief is." My priority is not to mislead anyone about the basis for my approach.

Section 9. Beginning the Work

Now that you are immersed in background about how things work, it's time to get into the training process itself. As you enter our training facility, you are greeted by the trainer or behavior consultant assigned to you. In many cases that person is me, Jim—also known as Dr Jim, Uncle Jim or Your Friend Jim as the dogs get to know me.

Your first chore, if not done previously, is to complete a behavior history and a liability waiver. The behavior history helps me understand the context for your dog's behavior. The liability waiver is reproduced below. The waiver is intended to be thorough. Please take a look; it is educational.

Waiver and Release

I. Participant Information_____

II. Liability Release

In consideration for Signature K-9 Behavior and Training LLC, Northern Legend Kennel and/or James or Charlene Akenhead allowing me, my spouse, or my child (or children) or those for whom I am guardian, and/or pets to participate in activities such as those described herein, I agree as follows:

1. This agreement, waiver and release apply to Northern Legend Kennel, Signature K-9 Services, James and Charlene Akenhead, as well as any

committees, employees, predecessors, successors, attorneys, insurers, as well as members, volunteers, officers, trustees, sponsors, share holders or board of directors of any group or organization (all of these are identified below as "Released Parties") who are working in the scope of their duties at the time of occurrence of any omission which is later alleged to be a cause or contribution to a claim for injury, damages or death.

2. I forever release, hold harmless and indemnify Released Parties from any and all liability, claims, suits, costs and attorneys, causes of action, damages, injuries or death to me, my minor children, any children under my supervision, my dog(s), my property, and legal liability of every nature, including negligent acts or omissions of any Released Parties, whether known or unknown, anticipated or unanticipated, direct or indirect, arising out of participation in the past, present, or future activities (including, but not limited to, activities such as visiting for entertainment; selection of a puppy, dog, or rescued dog; purchasing a dog; providing work or service in the kennel or with kenneled animals; while training my dog(s) or dogs belonging to others; while assessing dogs; while playing with dogs; while grooming dogs; when boarding dogs; or for any other activity). I assume all risks of injury or death as set forth in this release.

3. It is my express intent that this Waver and Release shall bind the members of my family, my spouse, and my estate, as well as my heirs, administrators,

personal representatives, or assigns, and shall be deemed as a Release and Waiver, Discharge and Covenant not to sue the above-named Released Parties, even if they engage in negligent conduct: and I make this agreement, Waiver and Release on behalf of myself, my spouse, my child and/or heirs, executors, administrators, successors, representatives and assigns.

III. Activity Risk

I understand that those involved in supervising or assisting with activities may not be professionals. I also understand that when working with or being around dogs there are numerous obvious and non-obvious inherent risks of serious injury or death, or property damage, to me or my dog, or others, which are always present in the type of activities noted herein. I acknowledge the information noted in section IV. Nature of Dogs, and understand that I am solely responsible for assessing my ability and confidence to participate in any activity and that I may decline to participate in any activity.

IV. Nature of Dogs

Although dogs are often thought of as honorable, loyal and trustworthy companions, I also understand that dogs, irrespective of training, may react unpredictably at times, based upon instinct or circumstances, including but not limited to: reaction to sounds, movements, unfamiliar objects, persons or animals; certain hazards such as surface and subsurface conditions; collisions with other dogs, handlers, or objects; participant negligence; as well as unpredictable or erratic actions by others and may become fierce, aggressive, vicious, or dangerous and may attack people without warning.

Further, it is recognized that any dogs present may not have received required or recommended vaccinations and that this represents additional danger of injury or death to my dog(s). Additional risks from dogs include, but are not limited to: dog fights, dog bites and injuries to humans and other dogs; dog theft or unlawful capture; dog escape over or under fences or through doors; plants and/or water sources; vegetation that may have burrs or seeds that could become tangled in a dog's coat or lodge in a dog's feet, ears, nose, or eyes; mosquitoes, ticks, chiggers, fleas or other insects, wild animals such as skunks, raccoons, opossums or stray dogs.

I also acknowledge that dogs may fail to respond to cues or commands; they may escape, or slip their collar; that dogs are faster than humans and may bite, change direction or speed, trip, slip, fall, stop short, shift weight, spook, or run if danger is perceived or if frightened or provoked. or for no obvious reason whatsoever. Finally, I understand that serious injury or death may result from working with or being around dogs.

V. Conditions and Nature of Locations
Released Parties have not inspected, and make no warranties concerning the safety or condition of any surface, site, building or other location of events or activities, including those in a private home.

VI. Emergency Treatment
I agree that the Released Parties are granted permission to authorize emergency medical treatment and I agree that I

am solely responsible for payment of any such medical treatment. I also understand that the Released Parties assume no responsibility for any injury or damage which might arise out of or in connection with such authorized emergency medical treatment.

I have read, understand and voluntarily agree to this four-page waiver and release. I further agree that no oral statements, representations or inducements apart from this written agreement have been made to obtain my consent. I further agree that this waiver, release and covenant not to sue shall remain in effect until revoked in writing by me. I also agree that should I revoke this waiver, release and covenant not to sue, I will no longer be able to participate in activities of the type represented herein and that the provisions of this agreement shall remain in effect as described for any and all activities or consequences of activities in which I have participated up to the date of the revocation.

Participant's Signature _____

If participant is under 18, the signature of parent or legal guardian signifies and represents agreement to the terms of this waiver, release and covenant not to sue on behalf of the minor and, if applicable per the specifications of participation noted herein, to him or her self.

The Complexity of Liability

The liability issue is complex. The waiver was designed after research into a variety of organizations and was reviewed by our attorney before we put it into use. The bottom line here is that dogs are living beings. There are no guarantees about their behavior—any more than there are guarantees about human behavior. You've surely heard stories about the quiet, seemingly nice neighbor who suddenly killed his family.

People need to be aware that there are no guarantees and that their personal commitment is going to be necessary if their companion is to become their partner in a solid relationship.

Case Example: Dog Evaluation
I have had the good fortune to attend several seminars by Dr. Pamela Reid. At one of those seminars, Dr. Reid presented video case studies of dog behavior evaluations. In one case, everyone in the room fell in love with the dog in the video. The dog couldn't be nicer. He did everything right.

The situation was a set-up. After a perfect evaluation using all kinds of activities to test the dog, later, when he was away from the evaluation setting, he attacked. He had such a severe reaction to a particular trigger that he had to be euthanized.

Dr. Reid's point, I believe, was that there is no foolproof evaluation system. My translation is that you can test a dog on 100 things; he may pass the first 99 and trigger at the 100th. For that reason, we must understand that we have a big responsibility when we take on a canine companion.

Also for that reason, I can not do an evaluation after a dog has bitten and assure the owner—or a court—that it will not happen again. Even so, many situations can be managed. That means a structure for life (which, if it had existed in the beginning, would likely have prevented the bite), a clear set of cues and behavior markers that have been carefully taught, and a commitment to make the plan work. In these cases, the future is really in the hands of the owner or handler of the dog. It can't be left up to the dog with the idea that if he is "trained," nothing will go wrong. The owner dare not become lackadaisical after months or even years of uneventful success.

Getting to Know Your Dog

While you complete the required forms at our training facility, I get to know your dog by walking her around the facility, letting her look in the corners and behind the desk to be sure there are no boogey men hiding in wait. (If the dog is scared or wants to bite me, I forgo this activity.)

During this exploration, I toss treats on the floor to see how the dog reacts. If the dog readily picks up the treats and looks to me for more, I suspect that the socialization process is on the right track. If the dog shies away, won't eat a treat, carries herself low or won't go with me at all, I begin to assume that socialization may need work.

Usually, there is time for me to test the dog to see if she will follow a lure into various positions. This is early preparation for teaching cues.

The Interview

After I get to know your dog, I get to know you. The process begins as I ask for an overview of the situation. I take notes about major issues and compare client comments with information on the assessment sheet that has been completed.

I ask questions that occur to me as we talk. My questions are often phrased as, "Exactly how, when, where, and with whom does this behavior take place?" My goal is to get precise details about the behavior and its context. Without these details, it is difficult to come up with a good plan.

Protocol: A Structure for Doing Things

When I have a feel for the basic information, I begin to work through my protocol—that is, I establish a framework of key elements that can help clarify the lifestyle of the dog in his family. Once this basic framework is in place, we make sure all specific problems identified by the dog's owner are accounted for. Often, at least some of the owner's problems are resolved as we put my basic framework in place. Later, when assessing how things are going, I recheck against both the protocol we put in place and the specific problem-solving we did. I often find that if problems continue, some part of the original protocol is not being followed.

For example, my protocol includes a process to stop jumping. It also involves a specific feeding process that helps establish various roles in the family. It supports everything else that we do. If a client tells me she is not using the feeding protocol, she has removed one of the support systems of my approach. If a client tells me the dog won't stop jumping and I ask what she is doing and she says, "I tell him to stop," I know there is a problem because that is not part of my protocol.

I find it easier to solve problems using a consistent protocol as a foundation, rather than isolating a single behavior, such as jumping, and trying to tackle it outside of any context. I often find that if problems continue, some part of my protocol is not being followed. If the protocol is being followed as explained and the behavior continues, we work more on problem solving to find the weak link.

Section 10. A Structure for Training

Explanation of Training Approaches

In a private training session, the first thing you hear from me is an overview of methodology similar to my explanation of traditional and contemporary training in Section 6. If you are paying attention, you quickly come to understand that my inclination is to use positive motivation as much as is possible. My way of stating this is, "We teach the dog that to get what she wants, she must give us what we want. We do that with a focus on rewarding behaviors we want rather than punishing behaviors we don't want."

An Indisputable Truth

There is one clear truth about people and dogs. It is that no one—absolutely no one—can prove that they can get into a dog's mind and tell you what the dog is thinking. At best, we can deduce what might be going on by comparing our version of a dog's behavior with conclusions made from research into dog behavior. Every step we take away from conclusive research makes our ability to diagnose and predict behavior a little fuzzier.

Good training and behavior work includes using research, considering the opinions of experts in the field (who do not always use research), and relying on our own intuition, hunches and gut feelings.

Positive Reinforcement

Positive reinforcement means giving your pet something pleasant immediately after she does something you want

her to do. That pleasant experience makes the dog more likely to do the behavior again. For best results, the pleasant experience (the reward) should show up within a couple of seconds after the behavior you want. For example, if you ask your dog to sit and the pleasant experience happens after she stands back up, she'll think she's being rewarded for standing up. She won't make the connection with the sit. This shows how timing your reward makes a difference in how easily and quickly the dog learns.

Positive reinforcement, your timely reward, can be anything the dog likes, including food treats, praise, petting, going outside, a drink of water, a favorite toy or a game. Food treats usually work well when training your dog. Food is what is called a primary reinforcer for the dog. That means you don't have to teach the dog to like it. You just have to find a food treat that the dog values.

Your training treat should be a small piece of soft food, so that your dog can immediately get it down and look to you for more. If you give her something she has to chew or that breaks into bits and falls on the floor, she'll be looking on the floor, not at you.

Small pieces of soft commercial treats, hot dogs, cheese, cooked chicken or beef all work well. Each time you use a food reward, you should pair it with a verbal reward (praise)... something like "Good Dog" in a positive, happy tone of voice. You could also reinforce the behavior with a toy or brief play. The reason I prefer food for initial training is that it's easier.

When you're teaching a new behavior, your dog should be

rewarded each time she does the behavior. This continuous delivery of reinforcement should be used until your dog associates the cue you use with the position you are cuing and the name (sound) you give it.

The Dog's Perception

Literally anything the dog likes that is okay with the owner can be used to reinforce a behavior. When using food, all you have to do is figure out what food the dog likes and you are holding all the cards.

The value of all treats or rewards is decided by the dog. You might think giving Cheerios is a great treat. Most dogs probably won't see it that way—although there are some dogs who seem to like breakfast cereals. We find that liver is highly valued by most dogs. Cheese is another treat that dogs seem to go all out for.

As owner and trainer, you pick the treats based on your knowledge of what your dog likes. If what you are asking the dog to do is easy and low stress, you can use lower value treats. If you are teaching the dog something new or asking him to do something that is hard for him, you would do well to use a treat that is high value to the dog.

Punishment

Punishment means your pet experiences something unpleasant immediately after she does something you don't want her to do. It can be verbal, postural (using body language), physical, psychological or biological. Effective punishment makes it less likely that the behavior will occur again. Technically, simply using the word "No" as a marker before doing something unpleasant to the dog can create an association in the dog's mind that the word "No" predicts something unpleasant is coming. Eventually, "No" itself can become the unpleasant thing. But in practical use, since my most common follow-up to the word "No" is to just ignore the dog—give no feedback—the word "No" does not need to mean something ominous in the dog's mind. To reverse think it, the word "No" simply means "nothing good will follow this behavior."

If you choose to use what I would consider active punishment (such as a swat or a collar correction), it must be delivered while your pet is engaged in the undesirable behavior—in other words, "caught in the act." If punishment is late, even seconds late, your pet may not figure out what behavior the punishment goes with. That causes frustration and fear in your dog. If your dog can't connect the punishment with a specific behavior, she may think you have gone crazy. Too much of this and your dog will be worried all the time about what you might do.

One downside of punishment: if the dog can directly connect an active punishment to you, it may erode your dog's trust. That's why punishment is most effective when it does not seem to come directly from you. For example, if you use a shake can or a horn, don't draw attention to the fact that the noise comes from you. Don't point the horn at the dog and threaten. An added plus is that if your dog perceives her "environment" to be the source of the punishment, she'll be more likely to avoid the behavior even if you're not around.

Guilty looks—as interpreted by humans—are actually

response postures. Animals may not have a human's sense of right and wrong, but they are good at figuring out that your presence, combined with a certain look, will likely lead to something unpleasant (punishment). Don't make the mistake of thinking this means the dog understands why you are upset. If your timing is not perfect, the dog may never figure out why you are upset. He just knows you are upset so he goes into an appeasement posture to say "please don't hurt me," because his only other options are to run from you or bite you.

Using physical punishment, such as holding the neck skin and shaking your dog or performing "alpha rolls" (forcing your dog onto her back and pinning her on the floor) can result in bites. When you do this, you force your dog into a corner—she must submit, struggle to get away or bite you. Many people assume that their dog will always choose to submit, but this is not so. If the dog chooses to fight and wins, you can be hurt and the problem has just been magnified. Another issue with physical punishment is that it can be associated with the people who are present at the time the punishment occurs. For example, a pet who is punished for getting too close to a small child may become fearful of or aggressive toward children.

Accumulating Chips

In his book on self-esteem, Jack Canfield described a concept called the "poker chip theory." Imagine a stack of chips with a value that changes each time you make a decision about how to respond to your dog's behavior. If your decision falls within a range that is acceptable to your dog, chips are added to the pile. Each time your decision falls outside that range, it costs one or more of those chips.

When comparing the pros and cons of positive approaches versus unpleasant approaches, being positive is what accumulates chips. Enough accumulated chips can provide a buffer for the inevitable uncomfortable decision. The chances of building a great relationship are higher when there are chips to cash in.

Fear and Feelings

In addition to the traditional and contemporary training approaches, more people are writing and talking about the place of thoughts and feelings in the lives of animals. In research with rats, some neuroscientists have speculated that animals have feelings of joy and unpleasantness. Yet, even with the emergence of feelings as a legitimate topic, some still hesitate to use the term. Instead, we hear phrases like "appears to be anxious." They are reluctant to commit to the idea that animals have real feelings.

For me, fear is a very significant issue when dealing with a dog's life. Fear can come from improper socialization, from a dog's genetic background, or from learning events involving humans, other animals or the environment.

Fear can make a dog's life miserable. When fear consumes a dog's life, everything is difficult for the dog. Many of the problems that require special help from a trainer or behavior consultant—even those that appear to be related to outward aggression—may stem from fear. Knowing this, it is important that our plans to help the dog do not increase the dog's fear or anxiety. The plans must include reduction of fear. In some cases, dealing with fear and anxiety involves the use of supplements or medication.

Socialization

Socialization includes adjustment to common occurrences in life, including dogs, people, places, objects and situations. Well-socialized dogs are more likely to have well-socialized puppies. Pups often mirror their mother's attitude. If that attitude or persona is anxious or fearful, puppies may pick it up. If genetics or assumption of the mother dog's attitude produces an anxious or fearful pup, socialization is very critical.

Puppies separated from littermates too early may also fail to develop appropriate social skills, such as learning how to send and receive signals, how far to go in play, and about "inhibited bites" (acceptable mouthing pressure). Play is important among puppies because it develops their physical coordination, social skills and learning. By interacting with their mother and littermates, puppies explore ranking (who's in charge) and also learn how to be a dog. Ideally, puppies should stay with their littermates for a minimum of seven weeks. Skills not acquired during this time may be much harder to acquire later in life.

Stages of Development

Based on structured observation in controlled settings (done by Drs. John Paul Scott and John L. Fuller and published in 1965 in *Genetics and the Social Behavior of Dogs*), dogs are thought to develop in identifiable stages. Listed below is one view of these stages. As more research and observation are conducted, interpretations or opinions of these stages may change.

- **Neonatal Period (0–2 weeks):** Puppies are most influenced by their mother.

- **Transitional Period (2–4 weeks):** Puppies are influenced by their mother and littermates. Eyes open, teeth begin to emerge, the senses of hearing and smell develop. Pups stand, walk, wag their tail and bark.

- **Socialization Period (3–12 weeks):** From three to seven weeks, puppies need chances to interact with other puppies and people in the safety of their litter while housed in a clean facility. At seven weeks or older, when puppies come to live in their new homes with humans, they need additional opportunities to meet other dogs and people. This is the time to ramp up opportunities for interaction.

- **New Home Socialization 7–12 weeks:** Puppies typically go to their new homes and begin a new phase of socialization. The key is to introduce them to experiences and people that are unlike those they encounter every day in their new home. Anything that is different from their home life will be of concern if pups don't learn early that different does not mean scary or untrustworthy. According to Ian Dunbar, if you could introduce your puppy to 100 people by the time he is 12 weeks old, it would not be too many.

- The same idea is true for places; take him places that are different from his home, such as a car wash, an elevator, strip malls, parks, anywhere he will experience different surfaces, sounds and feelings. Make it a point to think, Where can I take my pup that he hasn't been?

If socialization is not done, reconditioning, if possible, can require a huge commitment and can take a long time.

Meeting People

When your dog meets people, it must happen in a non-intimidating, non-threatening manner—from the dog's point of view. Remember, dogs and humans are different species. What we might think of as entirely harmless could have a different meaning in a dog's view. Generally, I like to associate a dog-human meeting with a high-value food treat. This sets up a positive association. The dog associates the treat with meeting new people... that's a good thing. If this is done regularly, over time it sets the dog up to look forward to meeting new people.

To ensure the new person does not appear to be intimidating or challenging to the dog, be sure that the person does not look directly into the dog's eyes. Also, have the person turn slightly sideways. Have them offer the treat in a flat hand at the person's side. If the dog is hesitant to come up and get the treat, use the breadcrumb approach: have the new person toss tiny bits of treat out to where the dog is and gradually lure the dog in by tossing the treats closer. Be patient. Keep this up until the dog is comfortable.

Do not let the new friend go to the dog. Let the dog move to the person. Keep new friends from leaning over the dog or reaching their fist out toward the dog. If your dog is nervous, it is very important that she does not feel forced to meet people. Take your time and use the breadcrumb approach.

Once the dog will take a treat from an open hand at the person's side on several occasions, move on to petting the dog, starting under the chin and neck, then along the side. If the dog backs up when petting is attempted, back off. Offer more treats until the dog is more comfortable. Be patient. Once the dog accepts petting under the chin, you can consider petting the head. Over-the-head petting is easier for the dog once he knows and trusts a person. If your dog does not respond to this approach, you may need help from a trainer. If you are not working with one, now is the time to start.

Rule of Thumb

A rule of thumb is that anything you want your dog to do as an adult is easier if it's introduced as a puppy. This can be seen in the so-called Superdog programs designed by breeders of dogs who work in the military, law enforcement, search and rescue and other high-demand occupations. In these programs, puppies are challenged by many experiences that are specifically designed so that a strong foundation of confidence is built.

One-Trial Learning

If a puppy or dog has been exposed to a traumatic experience, such as being hit by a car, kicked or exposed to very loud noise, that experience may make an indelible impression. That impression may drive her for the rest of her life. Overcoming a traumatic learning experience can require a big commitment from the dog's human partner.

Case Example: Electronic Collar

A series of traumatic or highly distressing experiences can also create a dysfunctional pattern of behavior in a puppy or dog. One example is the use of a shock collar when the dog has no idea why he is being shocked. What is typically said by the user of the collar is, "The dog knows, or should know, why he is getting shocked." My experience has been that many people who use shock devices are not clear with their dog. The dog has not been trained to understand what is happening.

To complicate matters, the human involved is often influenced by how he feels at any given time. For example, if he has a bad day, the dog may get shocked for things that he would not get shocked for if the owner was having a good day.

Another example might be the dog who runs away and, when she returns, gets a beating. Consider that... I come back, you beat me, and I'm supposed to want to come back. Or how about a dog who is on a "Down" cue when a child intentionally jumps on the dog's front legs. What do you think that dog's perception of kids might be? Traumatic experiences like these can become a strong influence in that dog's life.

Overprotection

I address this as a separate category because it occurs so often. When a dog seemingly wants to be with his owner at every moment, clings and whines when he's not getting attention, and is always rubbing against or pushing on his owner, the dog may be the product of overprotection. This overprotection can be reinforced by the owner who believes the dog loves him so much that he can't stand to be away from him. This is so good for the human ego that it can be hard to consider it is not good for the dog; it is actually the seat of a dysfunctional relationship.

When done while the dog is a very young puppy, it can be the basis for lack of socialization, which makes development of a balanced relationship more difficult. For best results, follow the guidelines in the socialization program earlier in this section or develop and follow a program designed jointly by you and your behavior consultant. Either way, make sure you are only reinforcing behaviors you want.

Housetraining High Points

Housetraining may or may not be a big problem for your dog. Some dogs seem to get it quickly, almost without effort. Others seem to take forever to figure it out. Some dogs are still not housetrained when they are several years old. This is a summary of information discussed during a typical consultation. It does not consider all possible problems.

Puppies and dogs seem to prefer to be clean; that is, unless they have been kept in a filthy environment while with their mother and littermates, or later when the breeder or seller takes over responsibility for keeping their quarters clean. Basically, if a dog has the opportunity, he will usually choose not to urinate or defecate where he eats and sleeps. If his quarters are too small and he is not given a chance to relieve himself outside or in another controlled area, he may have no choice.

Rituals and schedules are very important in housetraining. The more consistent the dog's schedule, the better things will go. Urinating and defecating are tied to eating, drinking, sleeping and exercise. Your housetraining project must consider all of these. See the sample schedule below for an idea of how these things relate to one another. If you offer food and water at regular times, it will help your dog go potty at predictable times.

How to Schedule
Most pups will need to urinate and defecate within 15 to 30 minutes after eating and drinking. Most will need to urinate immediately after waking up. Pups may need to go every hour and a half.

Sample Schedule
- 6:30 a.m.: Take your pup out on leash; use a signal such as "Hurry." When the dog sniffs, say "Good Girl." When she goes, make a fuss and give her a treat on the spot (not back in the house).

- 7:00 a.m.: Feed and water, walk pup, play with pup, return pup to crate. Pup should be confined or be with you at all times.

- 10:30 a.m.: Offer water, walk pup, play 15 minutes, return to crate.

- 12:00 noon: Feed pup, offer water, walk pup, play with pup, return to crate or keep with you.

- 3:00 p.m.: Offer water, walk pup, return to crate or keep with you.

- 5:00 p.m.: Feed pup, offer water, walk pup, socialize with pup.

- 7:00 p.m.: Offer water, walk pup, play with pup, return to crate.

- 10:00 p.m.: Walk pup, return pup to crate for night.

This is only a sample schedule. You can develop your own schedule to match your lifestyle. Use the sample for approximate times and intervals between activities. If you have trouble, the first thing to evaluate is your supervision; pups should not be left unsupervised. They are like human toddlers. They will make unfortunate decisions. They do not understand the importance of your house or your possessions.

If you can't figure out why your dog is still making mistakes, tighten up your supervision and chart his eating, sleeping, exercise, drinking, urination and defecation by times of the day. Include both accidents and planed potty breaks. This kind of chart can help you understand if your dog has special potty needs.

Confine your dog to a "den" (crate) where he won't want to relieve himself. His den should be big enough to stand up, turn around and lie down. If it is bigger than that, it won't work as well.

Use a consistent outdoor potty location—same times and same place. Your dog does not need a lot of room. Take him out on a six-foot leash to the same place each time. Urine smell from past visits will speed success. Use a cue to train the dog to go on command, such as "Hurry" or "Go Potty" (any simple cue will work). When you reach your chosen spot, give your cue.

When at his spot, don't play with the dog. Discourage the dog from unrelated activities. If he smells a flower, jiggle his leash and say "No, Go Potty." Use mild praise when the dog is sniffing or looking. Use more praise and treat immediately, on the spot, when the dog has urinated or defecated.

If you dog goes in the house, only immediate intervention does any good (your voice is usually enough). Just interrupt the activity. Then take the pup outside to finish and praise when he goes in the appropriate place. Rubbing his nose in mistakes is not effective. It may just cause the dog to do a better job of hiding the evidence. In spots where accidents have occurred, get rid of the odor quickly and completely. Use an enzyme cleaner. These cleaners are available at most pet supply stores. They are formulated to remove any trace of the smell, even when humans can't detect it.

Amount of Food and Water
Too much water and your dog can't hold it, too little water and he could become dehydrated. Feed and water in an area free from distractions. Put the food down for 15 or 20

minutes, then remove leftovers. See Section 11 for information on symbolic feeding.

Water may be offered after eating. Allow the pup to drink all she wants in 10 minutes. The amount of water a dog needs varies due to age, activity and temperature. If you have questions about the right amount of water, talk with your veterinarian. Once a dog is housetrained, water can be available at all times.

Age of Accomplishment

Usually, pups should be housetrained by four months of age. Young pups have only partial control over their physical abilities. As the dog ages, control increases. Supervision is critical while the dog is maturing and learning. If the dog has free run of the house, accidents will continue.

Older Dogs

If an older dog has a breakdown in housetraining, have your veterinarian determine if there is a physical problem. Urinary tract infections can cause problems for dogs in managing their urination. If the dog is found to be healthy, consider if there has been a change in the dog's food or if the food manufacturer has changed anything in their formula or preparation. Finally, return to the methods used to originally train the dog. Be sure to restart at a level where the dog can be successful. You might also want to consider a different food. See Section 11 for more information on feeding.

The Human-Canine Relationship

People have interesting beliefs about the relationship between dogs and humans. For some, the relationship can be summed up as, "The dog should do what I say because I say so." For others, it means bringing the dog up as you would a child. For still others, their dog is their baby. When asked what's in it for the dog, befuddlement often hits. It's as if that part of the equation has never been considered.

The Communication Gap

That's when I suggest that many of the issues between dogs and humans exist because **people tend to treat dogs like humans in furry suits.** They act as if the dog comes equipped to understand English and can follow complicated phrases and lectures about behavior. As a capper, some people believe that dogs should have the same value system as humans. Dogs should know that your carpet is valuable and your couch is new and should not be marred.

While the human is treating the dog as a human in a furry suit, the dog is looking back through dog eyes hoping the human will communicate as a dog might. All in all, an irresolvable dilemma—unless the human decides to step up and figure out how to **close the built-in communication gap that exists because we are two different species.**

To close this gap requires a clear structure created by the human for the dog. It means simple, clear, consistent cues and behavior markers used all day, every day. This is easy for humans to intellectualize and not so easy to implement. Almost every dog owner I have met acknowledges the issue when it is presented. Each nods in agreement. And yet, when communicating with their dogs, most continue to act as if they are humans in furry suits. This is a habit, and to break a habit requires commitment from the human partner.

Family Structure

For harmony to exist, like all family members a dog must understand his place in the family hierarchy. This means that even though we may love the dog, we cannot treat him as a human. This does not make the dog less in our eyes. It just speaks to the reality that dogs are different and for things to go well, we've got to recognize those differences and create the correct structure in our family.

This requires confidence and consistent adherence to a plan that follows specific protocols when giving food, water, affection and attention. It also includes using symbolic activities that may help establish leadership and bonding.

Section 11. Foundation Blocks

Leadership and Bonding

Leadership and bonding involve some symbolic processes. Some trainers don't subscribe to the value of the type of symbolic activities I suggest. My position is that in the absence of research to the contrary, they remain useful. Further, I use them because the concepts have worked in the vast majority of settings where I have suggested them.

Using these processes helps develop the family-dog relationship in a nonconfrontational manner. As a caution, remember that children are the least likely to be accepted by dogs as ranking members of a family group, and therefore may require special consideration or protection.

Symbolic Feeding

The idea here is to use your normal feeding process to provide a structure that keeps your dog healthy and helps her understand her place in your family.

First, a plug for condition-based feeding. This means you control the amount of food your dog gets based on her needs, not necessarily her wants. Like humans, some dogs will eat until they explode unless a structure exists to help monitor what is actually needed.

Quality and Quantity of Food

Proper quality of food includes consideration of the amount of food being supplied to the dog. Food is fuel. If there is too much fuel, the dog will need to burn off excess fuel beyond what is needed for his normal daily routine. The amount and quality of protein and fat are also important when considering the fuel in a dog's diet.

The proper amount of food contributes to the dog's overall health. Too much food can cause the dog to be overweight. An overweight dog may have a shortened life span, more health problems, and more pressure on hips, elbows and back. The amount of food a dog receives needs to be monitored and compared with his weight and general fitness.

Just because a dog acts hungry does not mean she needs or should have more food. Ask your veterinarian to show you how to evaluate your dog's fitness level. Usually it involves running your hand across the dog's rib cage and along the top of her backbone. You should be able feel her ribs without your fingers falling between them and you should be able to feel the tops of the vertebrae along her backbone.

If either the ribs or the backbone are lost in a layer of fat, it's time to put the dog on a diet. Your veterinarian can assist you in deciding how much to cut back on food. Keeping your dog fit requires discipline. You've got to know exactly how much the dog gets. It's a combination of how much food and how much exercise that determines your dog's fitness level. If your dog is overweight, you must cut one or increase the other. And don't forget to count in the treats you give as part of your dog's food allotment. For some dogs, every piece of kibble must be earned. Nothing is given free.

I suggest using a measuring cup with lines on it to portion

out your dog's daily allotment of food. I like the lines on the cup because it lets me measure more accurately. As my dogs' needs change because of exercise, seasons of the year or the amounts of treats I give, I adjust the amount of food I provide in their bowls.

Symbolic Feeding Procedure

Now to the process. Determine how many times per day you are going to feed your dog. Under normal circumstances, one or two times per day is fine. If your dog has special needs, or for puppies, more feedings may be appropriate. If you believe your dog may have special needs, talk with your veterinarian to get the best advice.

Once you have determined the number of times you will feed your dog, I suggest the following feeding protocol.

- Put your dog's bowl on a bench or table so he can see you prepare the food and place it in the bowl. This is a symbolic way to show you are the provider. If your dog lived on his own, he would spend most of the day searching for enough food to survive. He would understand that food is valuable and scarce. This providership ceremony makes a visual connection with you as provider of this valuable commodity every time the dog has access to food.

- Next, have out on your preparation table something symbolic that you can eat. It can be a vitamin pill, a jelly bean, two peanuts, a small glass of juice... it doesn't matter, it's symbolic. This is not about eating a meal before your dog eats. It's about stopping for a second after you fill your dog's bowl and eating your symbolic treat, then going on with the process. This action says to your dog that you have status, you make decisions. You don't have to do this part of the process every time you feed the dog. Do it more in the beginning of your relationship and then periodically (perhaps once or twice a week).

- Third on your protocol is to pick up the dog's dish from the table or bench, hold it about shoulder height and ask your dog to do something. This is a form of symbolic cooperation. The dog must show cooperation in order to get his food. This usually means something simple like "Sit" (assuming your dog knows what that cue means). Cue your dog to sit. Watch for your dog's rear end to hit the ground. This is the achievement of the "Sit" cue. As the rear hits the ground, say "Good Boy," as in "you did the right thing and I like it." Then immediately release the dog with your release cue—I use "Okay"—and put the food down for the dog to eat. Here is the way it looks and sounds: "Sit" (watch for rear to hit ground), "Good Boy" (you did the right thing), "Okay" (you are free to get up from your sit), put food down immediately.

- Leave the food down for a predetermined length of time— 15, 20 or 30 minutes. At the end of this time period, if the dog's nose is not in the food bowl, pick up the bowl and all traces of food until the next scheduled feeding time.

- But what if my dog doesn't eat? Shouldn't I give him another chance or leave the food down longer? Not unless your veterinarian has determined that your dog has special needs. Otherwise, your dog will soon adapt to the schedule. Don't weaken.

- But what if my dog won't sit? Stay calm and committed to the process. Do not repeat the cue. You are holding all the cards... his food. Wait as long as you can stand it. When you can't stand it any longer, say the word "No" (that's not what I want) and then repeat the cue "Sit." Again, wait as long as you can stand it. Repeat this process up to three times—four if you are a pushover for your dog. If your dog knows the cue and does not respond, put the food away until the next scheduled feeding time and repeat the process. The dog will get it.

- Repeat this phase of the process for four or five days, until you and the dog are comfortable. Then you up the ante. That means you are going to require more from the dog in order to get his food. You do the same symbolic preparation activities as before, then, when you pick up the bowl, hold it shoulder high, cue "Sit," wait for the rear end to hit the ground, say "Good Boy," then lower the food bowl about 10 inches *without* saying "Okay." This means the dog has not been released. If the dog holds the sit as you lower the bowl those 10 inches or so, say "Good Boy," then "Okay" and put the food down.

- If the dog moves while you are lowering the bowl (before you stop the bowl and release with "Okay"), say "No" (that's not what I want) and lift the bowl back up to shoulder height. Cue the "Sit," acknowledge with "Good Boy" and then lower the bowl again. If the dog holds still as you lower the bowl those 10 inches, say "Good Boy," use "Okay" for the release and let the dog eat.

- If the dog moves on the second, third or 10th attempt, calmly say "No" (in a conversational tone and level), move the bowl back to shoulder height, cue "Sit," acknowledge "Good Boy," and repeat the process. After this has been successfully mastered, repeat this step for five days or until the dog has it down cold.

- The next step is to do all the preliminaries and then lower the bowl from shoulder height down an arm's length. Repeat the same process as in the previous step. Do this part of the process until your dog has it down cold.

- The final step includes all the preliminaries and you lower the bowl all the way to the floor. Watch closely as you do this. The dog is more likely to break your "Sit" cue as the food gets closer to the floor. If he moves, say "No," move the food back up, cue "Sit," acknowledge "Good Boy" and lower the food to the floor again. When dog holds the sit until the food is on floor, release him to eat with "Okay."

Remember, you hold all the cards in this activity. There is no reason for you to give in.

On average, it's best if your dog gets just enough food to meet his needs. That means there should not be food left over after his meal time. The amount stated on the food bag is just a guide. Your evaluation of your dog's condition should control the amount you feed. If you are not sure, discuss the situation with your veterinarian.

Summary: This protocol sets you up as a provider with status, all accomplished without confrontation. It helps teach the dog to cooperate to get what he wants. The dog learns that food is scarce and valuable. Finally, the dog does a formal obedience sequence every time he is fed—all without physical manipulation. If anything about this process concerns you, contact a professional for advice.

Massage: Body Desensitization

Desensitizing your dog to handling can be greatly enhanced by doing regular massage. The goal is to get the dog to relax into the process of being touched. Remember, massage is different than play, brisk petting or brushing. The key is to cover **every inch** of the dog's body. Think of the massage stroke as a mother dog licking a puppy. Use enough pressure for the stroke to be comforting and go slow enough that the dog does not get excited and want to play.

Cover every inch of the dog. Do both sides of her mouth, over the bridge of her snout and forehead, go over both eyes, do both earflaps (carefully). Do all four legs... stroke down and slide off the paw. When the dog is comfortable

125

with this, cradle the foot before sliding your hand off the paw. After she accepts this, stroke between the toes. And finally, stroke the pads under the feet. Of course, stroke the main parts of the body, too; go down the chest and underneath from the front and around the rump and underneath from the back.

Do this massage daily for the first week or so with a new dog. After the dog is accustomed to the process and is easily relaxed, it can be done less often. I suggest doing a full body massage at least once a week—more if you like.

Do not shy away from any parts. Start in areas where the dog is less sensitive and most easily relaxed. Get the dog relaxed when stroking easily accepted parts of the body, then move to a more sensitive area, then right back to a more acceptable area. As you work with the dog, pay special attention to areas where the dog is sensitive, such as the feet and toes.

If you need to offer a special incentive for the dog to allow massage in sensitive areas, such as the feet, use a high-value treat like cheese or a ball of meat. When you move to the sensitive area, put the high-value treat in front of the dog's nose and let her lick it while you stroke the area. When you move to other areas, remove the treat. This does two things: it gives the dog something to focus on instead of worrying about the area being touched, and it also begins associating the massage with the presence of good things.

This process helps build a deeper bond between you and your dog. It desensitizes your dog in her skin—makes her less reactive if touched or bumped. The process also lets you inspect the dog for bumps, bugs and sensitive areas. Finally, it makes the dog less stressed at the veterinarian's office when being manipulated during an examination. As a byproduct, it makes life easier for your veterinarian.

Furniture and Beds

Some people believe that dogs can develop an attitude—even become aggressive—if they are allowed to get on beds, chairs, couches and other furniture whenever they want. Others will tell you that there is no research to prove this. In fact, some mention informal surveys where large groups of respondents have indicated that they have dogs on beds and furniture with no problem. To further complicate the mix, a behavior expert whom I believe to be among the top people in the country has indicated that her hunch is that some dogs may get an attitude if they are allowed up on the furniture on their own.

With this in mind, it is wise to consider that if dogs are given free rein with furniture and beds, it may lead the dog to perceive that he owns the territory thus claimed. As an example, when a dog is on a bed and a young child attempts to move the dog off, perhaps by pulling the dog's collar, if the dog assumes that he is entitled to be up on the bed he may also feel justified in disciplining the child for invading his space. Although this may not occur in all instances, the risk is worth considering.

Further, we are aware of other instances where, once a dog settles in with the perception of higher status and then connects that with resource guarding, he may refuse to move from his favorite chair or bed even when requested by an adult. A case comes to mind where a male Mastiff would not allow the husband to share the bed with him and the wife.

After the dog has been with a family for some time and his behavior is clearly predictable, it may be safer for you to consider allowing the dog up on the furniture. My suggestion to clients is to make a conscious decision about this. Don't just let it happen. If the decision is to allow the dog to get on beds, chairs or couches on his own, pay close attention to any questionable behavior that develops.

My personal preference is to either keep my dogs down or have them come up on cue or at my request. This means using a cue such as "Up," accompanied by a pat on the lap or cushion. When the dog gets up, you acknowledge with "Good Boy." When you are ready for the dog to get down, say "Okay" and move the dog off. With this method, if the dog gets on any furniture any time when he has not been not invited, tell him "Off" and remove him. Better yet, plan to make sure he doesn't get up unless invited. Be creative; this is not rocket science.

Section 12. Relationship and Structure

Formal and Informal Life

There is a difference between good manners and formal obedience. Both are important and both can be taught. A dog with good manners knows how to conduct his or her self in most social situations. A dog with good manners will need to spend less time in formal, non-negotiable obedience positions. Good manners can be taught with consistent application of behavior principles and a clear structure.

We are teaching our dogs all the time. It's important that we are clear about our expectations so we can reinforce them. Take time to get a clear idea of what you want from your dog. If you can't state your expectations, you are probably not clear in your own mind. If you are not clear, you will never be able to communicate your desires to your dog.

My personal definition of good manners is standing, walking, sitting and lying down, with no vocalizing (unless that's part of a specific strategy). That means 24 hours a day, seven days a week, we must pay attention to our dog's behavior and let him know what behavior we like and what we don't want. For me, this involves setting up two specific cues and using two different voice tones to mark behaviors. These cues are:

- **"No"** said in a normal, not screaming, not intimidating voice is used to mark behaviors that I do not want. I want the dog to learn to interpret the sound of "No" as simply "that's not what I want."

- **"Good Boy" or "Good Girl"** said in a different tone—happy if you like, Smurf-like if you can identify—is used to mark behaviors I like. I want the dog to learn to interpret this sound as "you are doing the right thing and I like it."

In our informal life, we don't impose too much on the dog except the expectation of good manners. If the dog volunteers to lie down beside me I tell her "Good Girl" and she is not required to stay in that position because I did not cue it (ask for it). Likewise, if my dog sits beside me voluntarily, she is not obligated to remain in a sit position. She can get up and move away any time she wants as long as she maintains good manners.

In our formal life, things are different. When we formally ask the dog to do something, we want to have established that the dog understands she should do what the cue requests and remain in the position requested until she is formally released.

Formal and informal context are very important. In the informal, the dog manages her own behavior, is acknowledged for the things we like, and no formal cues or releases are involved. In the formal context, the dog does as cued and remains as cued until officially released. Keeping these distinctions clear makes life and communication with your dog much easier.

Picking Cues

If you don't like my choice of words for these two types of feedback, pick your own. You could just as easily say "Goldfish" where I say "No" or "Gosh" where I say "Good Boy" or "Good Girl."

Our dogs don't come equipped with knowledge of English or any other language common to humans. It is our job to teach the dog what a given sound (which we call a word) actually mans. So again, you pick the sound and teach your dog its meaning. My only caution is to be consistent and don't get so fancy that you might forget the cue under pressure.

Case Example: Baseball

I once watched a handler work her dog in an obedience competition using only baseball terms. She used batter up, home run, first base, second base, etc., and the dog worked beautifully—I think maybe even to the tune of a first place in her division. You may also have heard of police or military dog handlers using a foreign language to cue their dogs. This may make it harder for others to influence the dog, because they don't know what cues were taught.

Consistency

By using uniform cues and two different, nonaggressive voice tones consistently, you give your dog feedback that helps him understand what you, as a human, want and don't want. Remember, you must teach your dog these things and make it worth his while to learn them. As a dog, he doesn't care about many things that are important to humans. He would actually prefer that we respond or react to him as another dog would react. He would prefer to roll in a dead rabbit than be sprayed with perfume.

What's in It for the Dog?

Many people believe that if I ask or "command" the dog to do something, he should do it without question or pause. I frequently hear people say, "I call my dog and she just looks at me like I don't exist." When I ask why the dog should come when called, some answer, almost in surprise, "Because I said so." As if it is genetically built into the dog or because the dog should see us as such a big prize that response is their only option.

If you think about this for a minute, you may begin to wonder what is in it for the dog in this kind of relationship. Why should she stop what she is doing just because someone said "come here"? The dog may be thinking, "Don't they know that there is a strong scent of a field mouse right here in the yard? Don't they know that my territory has been invaded by someone from outside?" Don't we know that the dog has her own autonomy?

The answer is yes! The dog does have independence about her. We humans are part of her life. We have some relationship with her and we have the opportunity to have a very significant and powerful relationship... but it takes some effort on our part. We have got to consider what's in it for the dog if she is to see us as better than the scent of a rabbit.

What this means, in most cases, is either we work with the dog from a traditional training sense, where the dog chooses to do what we ask in order to avoid being punished. Or we work with the dog in such a way that she chooses to do what we ask because she gets something she likes in return.

Do you know that if you are really good at punishment and your timing is close to perfect, you can actually teach a dog to act happy in order to avoid being punished? Wow! What a concept.

I know some may believe this is impossible and is a clear indication that I don't know what I am talking about.

But I assure you it's true, just as I assure you that punishment does work, and has worked for decades, if you are good at it and your timing is perfect. Don't get me wrong... just because it's true doesn't make it right!

Again, the choice is what kind of relationship you want with your dog. Do you want it to be based on punishment and intimidation or do you want it to be based on mutual enjoyment? For me, it seems there has been some higher power involved in bringing dogs and humans together. I often wonder why dogs would want to be as close to us as they are. Even though we are supposed to be the more highly evolved of the two species, the treatment that humans give dogs is often horrendous. They offer us the opportunity for great relationships and we return the favor with selfishness. We tie them to a post, exposed to sun and rain. We forget to fill their water dish. We let their coat get matted and covered with burrs. And when we call, we expect them to come because it's us. Wow!

Basic Training Equipment

As a convenience to our clients, we sell the equipment we use and demonstrate. This enables us to help diagnose what is needed and then try out the equipment on your dog. Listed below is the typical equipment our clients have seen being used. I make it a point to educate clients about equipment and its uses. We prefer working with a six-foot leash and a flat collar. If the dog is a larger breed, we like the old-fashioned buckle collar because we think it is the most secure. When working on leash walking, we encourage work with a flat collar first to see how much progress can be made. If progress is not as desired, we move to power steering devices.

I have listed several types of power steering devices. These apparatus help keep the dog from pulling while learning. We favor the specially designed chest harness for dogs who pull. These harnesses are usually accepted by the dog without much fuss. The head harness is my preference for a dog who pulls and throws in a lot of head action. This apparatus works well and usually requires about a 20-minute process to begin desensitizing the dog.

Leashes and Long Lines

Leather, nylon, cotton, chain cable and rubber-coated materials are used for leashes, lines and tethers. We like leather as a training leash because of its positive, comfortable feel in the hands. Oh, by the way, never leave leather alone with your dog or it will likely become a chew toy.

Nylon is strong but not as comfortable in your hands.

Occasionally we suggest nylon-coated cable as a drag line or tether for a puppy who chews. Cotton lines are comfortable, light and less durable than nylon. Chain should be avoided as a leash. Parachute chord is great for long lines. A six-foot leash is usually used to begin training. Six feet allows enough length to work away from the dog as he improves.

Harness

A harness is sometimes used because owners believe that a dog will choke himself on a neck collar. Unless specifically designed as a walking control harness, dogs may actually pull harder when a traditional harness is used. The Easy Walker and Halti Harness are specially designed to get a less agitating walk.

Head Halter

Two common head halter brands are Halti and Gentle Leader. They are applied to the snout and head like a horse halter. They are effective because they provide maximum leverage and head control for the handler. Head control can be an issue with reactive or aggressive dogs. Dogs may fuss about having something on their snout and desensitization is usually required. A DVD may come with the head halter to teach you how to desensitize your dog.

Flat Collar

Flat collars are generally considered a safe and humane tool for leash walking or tethering a dog. They have plastic clips or metal buckles and are usually made of leather or nylon. This is the only collar I would consider leaving on my dogs when I am not with them.

Limited Slip Collar

Sometimes called a Martingale collar or Greyhound collar, the partial slip collar can be made of nylon, chain or both. This collar is sometimes used because of the limited slip feature, which helps prevent dogs from slipping the collar (when they have a big neck and narrow head). They may help with control, too, but stop short of allowing the handler to choke the dog.

Slip Collar

These are available in chain of variable size links, as well as in nylon and leather. Slip collars are often called "choke collars" because, if used inappropriately, the dog can be choked. Dogs should never be tethered by a slip collar and slip collars should not be left on unsupervised dogs.

There is a correct and an incorrect way to wear and use a slip collar. This collar is often used incorrectly. Most people seem to believe that this collar is designed so that when the dog pulls, he chokes himself and that stops him from pulling. This is not correct. The slip collar is a difficult tool for most handlers to use and it is usually associated with the use of punishment as a training technique.

Prong or Good Dog Collar

Made with metal or plastic prongs on the inside and somewhat ominous looking, these collars close slightly when the leash is pulled. This causes a pinching effect. Some people believe this collar mimics a mother dog's teeth as used to discipline puppies. These collars are sometimes used for dogs who need a form of "power steering."

Prong collars can be misused and are often seen as undesirable. In spite of their appearance, these collars are still used in training some assistance dogs. When they are used, they are often seen as a way to help neutralize the physical strength of the dog versus a person with a handicap or someone who needs support because of their age.

Electronic Collars

Variations of these collars use sprays, vibrations, audible signals or electric shock as ways to affect behavior. Some of these may be useful when appropriately matched to specific behavior circumstances, under proper supervision. It is not appropriate to buy an electric collar and start shocking a dog when he does something "wrong." A clear behavior strategy should be used with any of these tools. In some cases, these collars can make behavior worse.

If the dog associates a shock with a particular person or classification of people (such as children), the dog may become more anxious or aggressive around them. Dogs can even seem to become "schizophrenic" with misuse of these devices.

Extreme caution is recommended. Do not use these devices without help from a certified trainer or behavior consultant. If you are told by one of these people that you should not be using this kind of device, I would follow the recommendation.

Is the Clicker Quicker?

Today's dog books are full of ideas about developing thinking dogs. That really interests me. I believe this is the wave of the future. In that paradigm, there are those who believe that the clicker is the best mechanism to teach a dog to think.

The clicker makes a noise like the cricket toy that some of us played with in the 1950s. It is usually about two inches long, an inch wide and one-half inch deep. There is a metal or plastic button that is pressed to get the click sound.

So, what makes the clicker magic? The magic of the click sound is that it can be delivered very quickly to acknowledge behavior and it does not carry the emotion that may be in a human's voice or body language. As a signal to the dog, it's very efficient.

The clicker is a good training tool. We use it when teaching certain complex behaviors that must be formed by connecting smaller pieces. We also use it with dogs who are so aggressive or so afraid that we can't get near them when we begin our work.

The clicker itself does not change behavior. It is only a vehicle for change. People can become very confused about this. One of our clients, fresh from an obedience class elsewhere and not satisfied with the result, made an appointment to see if we could help. When she entered our facility, she started clicking. When I asked about use of the clicker, she said, "I think it's supposed to calm the dog down."

When used correctly, the clicker can be a fantastic tool. In many cases, a well-trained handler can use their voice and body language to get good results without a clicker. If you want more information about clicker use, I suggest Karen Prior's web site (www.clickertraining.com) and her book *Don't Shoot the Dog*. Prior is the guru of the clicker.

Section 13. Context for Training

Prevention, Management and Training

As a dog owner, you are always responsible for preventing unwanted situations, managing those that happen by surprise (not because you were not thinking ahead), and providing training so that your dog can function in a human world. If you don't do these things, your dog's life is at stake—either because of a mistake that appears to be aggression or a mistake that ends up with the dog running away to be caught in a trap, killed on the road or shot by a disgruntled human.

In addition to your responsibility for your dog's life, you are at considerable risk from a liability standpoint. If your dog harms another or destroys property, it can cost you big money. If you are insured, it can cause cancellation of your insurance.

Creativity and Planning

In short, dog owners need to be creative planners. Dogs need guidance in a human world. Humans must provide that leadership. It can't be left to chance or a lackadaisical approach. For dogs and humans to have a good relationship, the human must consider it important enough to think about and plan for.

If you pay attention to your dog's behavior, you can become able to predict unwanted behaviors and the situations that trigger them. Your job is to be creative and come up with ways to prevent those trigger situations.

Case Example: Welcoming Guests

When guests come to your house, does your dog jump on them? If so, and if you know this in advance, are you planning a way to prevent the unwanted behavior? If not, you are allowing the behavior to become stronger with each rehearsal.

Creative planning in this case could be as simple as putting your dog on a house leash before welcoming your guests. This strategy may not be the ultimate solution to the problem, but it may be the perfect solution early in the process.

Case Example: Stealing Food

Does your dog counter surf? Steal food? Stick her head in the kitchen trash? Do you know ahead of time that this is likely to happen? If you do, you are creative enough to find preventive solutions that are either permanent or for short-term use while a better training solution is being designed.

Managing the Environment

The dog owner is responsible for the environment where the dog lives and visits. In today's world, dogs cannot understand or anticipate all of the factors that may be dangerous to them or in which they are dangerous to others. When the dog is young, immature and not fully trained, it's important to think ahead and use prevention and management. Don't wait until an undesirable situation occurs; you are in trouble at that point.

Dogs as Environment

For your dog, everything she experiences is part of her

environment. Everything! That includes other dogs and their handlers. This realization carries with it more responsibility. Any movement of another dog may be noticed by your dog, especially if she is continually scanning (checking out movement).

Whether you are taking a walk or attending a training session, other dogs become part of the environment that affects your dog. Sometimes this environment changes quickly. Other times a dog is so much a part of the environment that we can become desensitized to his presence—resulting in our lack of attentiveness. At this point, all it takes is an eye lock or a bump and the result can be very uncomfortable for all.

Combine the aforementioned realities with the fact that many dogs don't have the skills to meet another dog without causing a reaction, and the owner's responsibility is even heavier. If you add to all this the belief of some humans that all dogs should get along, the problem is magnified even more.

This means that you as a dog owner must take personal responsibility to manage your dog so that she does not get hurt and does not cause harm to another. Always know what is going on in the environment, even at your training school. Think ahead. Move your dog to areas that you can control. Condition your dog to focus on you when necessary.

Rehearsing Behavior
Prevention and management are important because every time a dog completes a behavior, it is a rehearsal. Every

rehearsal makes the behavior stronger. We don't want our dogs to rehearse unwanted behaviors. This is enough reason to carefully think ahead about the situations we will take our dogs into. Consider what might happen, how your dog will react and how you can plan carefully to prevent behaviors you don't want.

Three Ways We Relate to Dogs

There are essentially three ways we affect a dog's behavior:

1. Reinforcing the dog by adding something he likes.

2. Punishing the dog with something he doesn't like.

3. Neutral behavior that gives the dog no feedback at all.

As humans, it seems we prefer to love them or hit them. If you subscribe to the same value set that I do, you would not be in favor of hitting them. So in many cases, it seems like all you can do is love them, no matter what. But that isn't true! Neutral behavior, also known as **Ignoring Behavior**, is a good tool to use with your dog.

Unfortunately, in the human world, neutral behavior isn't often considered. But neutral behavior gives the dog something to compare to positive or pleasurable behavior. This gives us the option of rewarding the dog when he does something we want, ignoring the dog when he is giving us something we don't want, and not having to punish him.

I know, the first question here is what to do when the dog misbehaves. The inclination for many is to punish.

The problem with punishment, as explained earlier, is that it has a fairly big down side. My approach is to use prevention and creativity to manage situations so they do not become dangerous, and then ignore the dog when he offers behavior we don't want and that is not dangerous.

In this system, we reward the dog immediately when he gives what we ask for and we act as if the dog doesn't exist when he doesn't. The ignoring is neutral behavior. You are now probably asking yourself, How does ignoring or using neutral behavior cause the dog to behave better?

Case Example: The Jumper

Let's say your dog is a jumper. He comes out of his crate in the morning and jumps all over you. Of course, he's just excited to see you. When you get home from work, he jumps all over you as he greets you. You know it's all because he is excited about seeing you. And it is also a great ego boost to have a dog who acts like you are the number-one person in the world. That is the very reason why ignoring or using neutral behavior (remember that means **no feedback at all**) can work to get behavior change.

So here's how it goes: The dog thinks you are the greatest thing going, the sun rises and sets on you. He may even consider you a godlike creature as he looks at you through his dog eyes. Much of his life is focused on getting things he wants from you, including your attention and affection. Everything he does makes perfect sense to him, as a dog. Everything he has done and continues doing is being done because he gets something from it, and to date, this is the best way according to your dog's experience.

Maybe you have yelled at him when he jumps. Maybe you have kneed him, stepped on his toes (all punishment, by the way) or perhaps you have pushed him down or away. Yet he keeps coming back. So what does that tell you?

First, your plan isn't working! Maybe it isn't working because dogs are very tough. When we push or pull or hold them down, unless we get really nasty—nastier than most people are willing to get with their pet—the dog may see it as a game. It can be a very rough game and the dog may still be saying "bring it on." If you doubt a dog's toughness or ability to play rough, just watch two large dogs play together. They body slam, pull each other down and roll around much more than would be comfortable for most humans.

So, what do you have to loose by trying neutral Ignoring Behavior? It gives the dog a taste of what it's like not to get something he wants from you, it takes away the need for you to confront your dog, and it teaches your dog that he gets what he wants by giving you what you want. Okay, so how do you do it?

The answer is, Whenever the dog jumps up, you say the word "No," which means "that's not what I want," and then you symbolically go away.

- That means you close up your body by folding your arms, you turn your head to the side (no need to turn all the way around), you close your eyes and you stand perfectly still, no matter what the dog does.

Your dog may be astounded. The first thought that

probably goes through his head is, "This always worked before, so I guess I will have to try harder." You see, it makes no sense to your dog that you have stopped giving him attention for a behavior that has always worked before.

- So he begins to work harder. He may jump higher, jump faster, run around you and jump, bark at you and jump, jump up and paw at you, anything he can think of that might get your attention back on him.

You must hold out. No matter what your dog does to try to get you to pay attention by jumping, you ignore him. **No feedback**, only Ignoring Behavior.

- If you can hold out, one of three things will happen: a light will go on, he will get frustrated or he will get tired.

- It does not matter which, because at that moment, the dog will stop the jumping... if only for a second and if only to look up at you like it's you who doesn't know what you are doing.

- **At that second**, stop ignoring and say "Good Boy" (which means "you are doing the right thing and I like it") and pet the dog.

- As you do that, expect that the dog will immediately jump again. As soon as he does, you mark the behavior with "No" (that is not what I want from you) and do your Ignoring Behavior—fold your arms, turn your head to the side, close your eyes and don't move.

- Hold that position until the dog stops again. As soon as he stops, say "Good Boy" and pet him or give him a treat, or both.

- If he jumps, ignore; when he stops, make a fuss. Always mark the change with either "No" or "Good Boy."

- Be so consistent that the dog eventually gets that when he lifts his feet to jump, he never gets anything. When he keeps his feet on the ground—sitting, lying down or standing, and not vocalizing—he gets all kinds of attention.

Always observe your dog's reaction to your behavior. When you say "Good Boy," how does your dog respond? Does he stay down when you say "Good Boy" and jump or become agitated when you pet or touch him? Be aware of these kinds of reactions and adjust your actions to get the behavior you want from your dog.

Ignoring, or using neutral behavior and marking it consistently when the dog gives behavior you don't want will teach the dog how to know what you like, and further, that being ignored is not fun. You can handle any non-dangerous behavior this way. If the dog whines at you to get attention, ignore him until he is quiet. If the dog barks at you to demand your attention, ignore him until he stops.

Seems dramatic, doesn't it? It is. The Ignoring Behavior, as explained here, is intended to be dramatic. That is because the dog is a better body language reader than we are. This dramatic approach sends a blunt, clear message. After the dog becomes familiar with your use of the Ignoring Behavior, you will be able to simply say "No," shift your head slightly to the side, and the dog will know what you mean.

Self-discipline and consistency are the keys to success. If the dog annoys you by nipping at your pants leg, you can scream and fuss with the dog or you can maintain your Ignore until the dog loses interest. The first will encourage the dog to keep going; the second will teach the dog to stop.

For some people, the thought of a dog nipping at their pants leg is a big deal. Others worry that if the dog jumps and they are wearing shorts, their leg could get scratched while they are doing the Ignoring Behavior.

The solution here is the ability to plan ahead. If you are watching your dog, you will be able to predict when he is likely to jump or nip. If you can prevent it, do that. If the situation doesn't accommodate prevention, prepare yourself. Until your dog is trained, don't wear shorts if you know the dog will jump on your leg.

Case Example: All Dressed Up

One of our clients who owns a Chesapeake Bay Retriever was used to being mugged every day when she came home from work. The excited dog would meet her and jump all over her. As it happened, the client was required to wear dress clothing to work. Our strategy for dealing with this situation was that she would take sweat pants and an old heavy jacket with her to work. When she pulled into her driveway, she slipped the sweats and coat over her dress clothes before going into the house. The dog mugged, the client Ignored, the dog learned, and she now does not need the sweats and coat.

This may not be your choice for a solution, but you must admit it was creative and it worked. Another solution might have been to have her spouse put the dog in a crate 20 minutes before she got home and then let the dog out of the create after she was home for 20 minutes and the dog had settled down. Either might be effective.

Section 14. Fundamental Cues

Obedience training is usually thought of as mastering a series of commands that indicate what behavior we want the dog to do, combined with a release cue that tells the dog when he can stop doing what was requested. These commands usually include "Sit," "Down" and "Come." These cues enable the dog to work in a structured situation when required.

The Cue and the Action

Remember, any cue you use is just a sound to the dog. It's not about English, it's about a specific sound that we and the dog come to associate with a behavior and a result. It doesn't matter what you use as long as you use it consistently. The dog can learn whatever behavior she can physically perform that you can connect with a specific sound and a pleasant outcome.

When teaching a cue, either verbal or with another signal, our goal is for the dog to complete the action—that is, to sit and maintain that position until she either hears a release cue (such as "Okay" said in an upbeat tone) or until she hears another cue she understands.

Do You Need a "Stay" Cue?

You'll notice in my list of cues at the beginning of this section that I mentioned nothing about using the sound "Stay." Here is my rationale: Have you ever asked your dog to sit when you expected him to immediately stand back up?

When I ask that question, most people get a bewildered look on their face and, after a few confused seconds, say "No." If that is true, and if "Stay" is to be a useful cue, you would have to say "Stay" immediately after using any stationary command. This means every time you cue a sit, it would require you to cue "Sit, Stay," even if you wanted the dog to sit for only a few seconds.

So if one cue will do, why complicate things by using two cues? Instead, why not teach just one cue that means to assume the position and remain in the cued position until released by a clear release cue (such as "Okay") or by another cue the dog understands (such as "Down").

When they think about it, most of our clients conclude that "Stay" is not needed.

Release Cue, "Okay"
A clear release cue helps the dog to understand when he is finished, done or off duty. I like the word "Okay" as a release cue. I say it with enthusiasm and something of a lilt in my voice. Some people don't like "Okay" as a cue because they believe it is too close to a conversational use of okay and that the dog may be confused and release accidentally when hearing the word used in general conversation. I have not had that experience, probably because I use body language and an identifiable voice tone along with my "Okay" release cue.

That being said, the release cue can be any sound that you can use smoothly and are comfortable with. Some other possibilities are "Free Dog" or "All Done." Remember, any sound can be connected with any behavior if you teach it that way. The word you choose is not important.

What is important is that without a clear release cue, your dog must try to figure out on his own when he is done. Is he released when you smile, say "Good Dog," move away, wave your arms? He must study you and hope he doesn't make a mistake. For the dog's sake, pick a clear release cue and use it consistently in all situations where you ask the dog to do something for you.

"Wait" Cue

"Pause where you are until I say Okay" is how I use the cue "Wait." When my dog is about to exit my vehicle, I step in front of the door and say "Wait." After the dog settles down, I say "Okay," move away from the door and let the dog out. I use the "Wait" cue any time I want a temporary pause. When necessary, I use my body to block movement as I say "Wait." After a while, my dogs pick up the meaning and the cue becomes easy.

"Good Girl" and "Good Boy"

Completing a cue successfully needs an acknowledgement, a clear sound that means "you did it" or "you did the right thing... and I like it." I like to use "Good Girl" or "Good Boy" as my acknowledgement/reinforcement sound. My goal is to say the sound immediately when the dog completes the cue. For example, if I cue a sit, I say "Good Boy" the instant I see the dog's rear end hit the ground. The rear hitting the ground is the culmination—the end result—of the position I asked for and I want to give that a clear acknowledgement signal.

The Reinforcer

Reinforcing something means doing something immediately after a behavior that increases the chances the behavior will be repeated. For example, if my dog sits and I give him a bit of food, my dog is more likely to sit when he is around me. If, every time he sits he gets a piece of cheese while no other behavior gets him anything he likes, sitting will become a big deal for the dog. He will likely volunteer to sit all over the place to get cheese.

Primary Reinforcers

Food, treats, water, going to potty, all these are primary reinforcers. That means you don't have to teach the dog to like them or want them. It's natural. The reason I use food as a reinforcer is because it's easy. Dogs like food. The only puzzle is to find out what treat the dog likes best and to use the treat when the dog is likely to be interested or hungry—like not right after a meal of roast beef.

Secondary Reinforcers

Something the dog is taught to like is a secondary reinforcer. The dog is usually taught to like the secondary reinforcer by having it paired (combined) with a primary reinforcer over time. A typical secondary reinforcer could be your voice saying "Good Boy." It becomes a secondary reinforcer by being combined with something the dog likes.

Again, an easy example is food. If, every time I say "Good Boy" I give the dog a piece of food within a few seconds, eventually my voice begins to be of interest to the dog. After the combination of "Good Boy" accompanied by a treat occurs over and over again, my use of "Good Boy" alone will serve as a reinforcer—something pleasant to the dog. Hence, my voice saying "Good Boy" is likely to encourage the behavior that came immediately before it.

Variable Reinforcement

If I give my dog cheese every time he sits, he is getting continuous reinforcement. If I give my dog cheese four times out of every five times he sits, he is getting intermittent or variable reinforcement. Sometimes he gets reinforced and sometimes he doesn't. It varies.

Usually, I recommend using continuous reinforcement when teaching a new behavior. Then as the dog gets the behavior down pat, we switch to variable reinforcement. When we do this, we have to keep the dog guessing about when he will or will not get the reinforcer—often, a food treat.

Random Treating

A less technical way to refer to variable reinforcement is random treating. It's important to give the treat often enough that your dog will think it's worth it to keep working.

Not letting the dog know when he will or won't get a treat is also essential with random treating. To make it work, you must look exactly the same when you are going to give a treat as when you are not going to give a treat. If you somehow convey with your posture, how you hold your hands, the look on your face or the absence of a treat bag rattle that no treat is coming, your dog will figure it out and may not perform when you cue him.

Nickel Slot Players

When we use random treating, we want our dogs to be nickel slot machine players. People play nickel slots because they believe they have a high probability of winning. With nickel slots, you can keep playing without a high risk of loss and with a perceived good chance to win. With our dogs, random treating means they win when they get the treat and do not experience unpleasantness when they lose—don't get reinforced.

Expected Hits

How many hits, rewards or getting the treat must the dog receive to keep him working? Not as many as you may think. I start with a treat for every repetition when I am teaching a new skill. As the dog learns or associates the cue sound and the behavior, I begin to reduce the number of treats.

I do it in an organized way so I can tell if performance suffers. I might start with eight treats in my hand for a 10-repetition practice. I distribute the eight treats over the 10 repetitions in a random manner. If performance stays up, I may move to six or seven treats for 10 repetitions. I may continue this process until the dog can perform 20 repetitions with only one or two treat rewards.

If you are slowly lowering the number of treats and you reach a point where your dog's performance drops off, be sure you are not telegraphing treat versus no treat. If that is not the problem, up the treats to a frequency that brings his performance back. Then slowly move to reduce the treats again.

Your Part

It's not just the treat rewards that reinforce the dog's performance. It is your personal reaction. Do you get excited at the right time? Do you use your voice and body to generate enthusiasm? Do you mange your voice and your body so that they work in your favor?

Everything you do influences your dog's reaction. Some things are enjoyable for your dog, some things are neutral and others make the dog uncomfortable. You must become a good enough reader of your dog's body language to know how you are affecting him. You need to be aware that if you touch him he might not be able to focus, and if you get too excited he can't concentrate. You learn this by paying attention to your dog's reactions. Finally, when cuing your dog, you can't telegraph what reward he will get... or not get.

The Rattling Treat Bag

When training your dog, if as you give your dog a cue he hears you reach into your treat bag and rattle around for a treat, he knows what's coming. Likewise, if you cue him and he hears no rattle of the treat bag, he knows what's not coming. Even more obvious is if you wear a treat bag when doing formal training and not when out on a walk, the dog definitely knows the difference. This can affect performance.

The game for you is not to give yourself away. Notice how you hold your body. Where are your hands? Are you conveying things to your dog that are not included in your cue? Generate the same enthusiasm and body energy whether you are giving a treat or not. That will affect the dog's performance. He will be a more consistent nickel slot player.

The Lure

Interesting the dog in following a lure, in this case a treat, is done so that when we use a lure to teach a position the dog will easily understand and follow.

Orienting the dog to a lure is a simple process. For me, it means walking the dog around a room and periodically dropping a treat on the ground for the dog to find. At first, the treats are dropped in front of the dog's nose or right on top of the dog's head so she can't help but notice. As the walk continues, I drop the treats so the dog sees the treat bounce but must search a little to find it. If the dog doesn't find the treat, I point to it and guide the dog.

This process sets the dog up so she will follow a treat when it is used for a more deliberate activity, such as teaching "Sit" or "Down."

"Sit" Position

Perhaps the easiest cue to teach is "Sit." The sound "Sit" usually means the dog puts his rear on the ground and stays there until you release him or give another cue that he understands.

Remember, even the simple "Sit" cue is only a sound to the dog. It only means something when the dog associates it with a particular movement. For this reason, it is not necessary to say the word "Sit" while you are teaching the dog to follow a lure into the sitting position. It is only **after** the dog will consistently follow the lure that you start adding the "Sit" cue just before you start your luring motion. After a few practice sessions, the dog will begin to associate the cue with the movement into the sit position. At that point, you can fade the lure.

Fading the lure means making it less obvious as you use the verbal cue. Make the lure motion less and less obvious each time you do it... shorten your arm stroke and make the presence of the treat less and less visible. Later, you may use the motion you made with the lure as the basis of a hand signal. Ultimately, you may want your dog to respond to a verbal cue, a hand signal or a combination of both.

The "Sit" cue is relatively easy to teach because the dog can easily be lured into the sit position. Take a delectable treat, hold it just above the dog's nose and move it toward the dog's tail. As you move the treat backward, the dog's rear end naturally goes down as the head follows the movement of the treat. The instant the dog's rear hits the ground, you say "Good Boy," let the dog have the treat, and then quickly release the dog using "Okay" accompanied with a quick body shift to the side to get the dog up. This quick sequence gets the dog in position, acknowledges he did it correctly, rewards him and gets him up with a release before he gets up on his own.

"Down" Position

When your dog can sit on cue, the next move is to teach the "Down" cue. We use the "Sit" as the platform for the "Down"... meaning, we start the dog in the sit position and move him to the down position. One definition of "Down" (not used in formal competition) is simply to get the dog into a reclining position with his belly on the ground. The dog can role his hip into a relaxed position as long as he remains reclining.

Our goal is to teach the dog that when he hears the sound "Down," he puts his body in a reclining position with his belly on the ground. Further, we want to teach the dog that he remains in that position until he hears either his release cue or another cue he understands. (As a reminder, "Stay" is not a necessary cue for this process.)

- Don't bother to say the word "Down" when you first begin. Remember, dogs don't understand English until we teach them the meaning of the sound. In this case, we want to first teach the dog to mechanically move into the down position.

- When we can get the dog to follow our treat lure into the down position and we are sure the dog will continue to do so, then we start adding the "Down" cue just before the lure motion so the dog can associate the cue and the mechanical motion of going into the down position.

The mechanics of the down are simple. First, get the dog into a sit, either by asking for it with the cue or waiting until the dog sits. Remember, if you ask for the sit, you should acknowledge it with "Good Boy."

- Once the dog's rear end is on the ground, take a treat (I use a meatball-size lump of soft treat material) and put it under the dog's nose. As soon as the dog takes notice, start moving the treat clump slowly toward the ground. Go slow enough that dog can follow but fast enough that the dog can only sniff and lick.

- As the dog follows the treat clump toward the ground, reinforce with the sound "Good Girl." We use "Good Girl" as a reinforcer because the dog has become familiar with the sound as part of learning the "Sit" cue.

- Once the treat reaches the floor, slowly move it outward along the floor and away from the dog's nose. Again, go slowly enough that the dogs stays interested. The dog should slowly walk herself into the down position.

If the dog lifts her rear end off the floor as she follows the treat, quickly say the word "No" (as in "that's not what I want") in a conversational tone and move the treat away from the dog. Have the dog sit and begin again. Remain calm; if you are frustrated, the dog will pick up on this and become anxious. This will inhibit progress.

- Continue the process until the dog walks herself into the down position while following the treat. When the dog's belly touches the floor, say "Good Girl" and be sure the dog is getting the treat... actual bites. Continue treating and saying "Good Girl" for a few seconds, then remove the treat as you say the "Okay" release cue and get the dog up with a quick movement of your body.

If the dog does not follow the treat, you are either moving too fast or your treat is not of sufficient value to the dog to hold her interest. If she has just eaten a big meal or if there are distractions, it would take a very high-value treat to keep the dog's interest. If this is the case, take note and adjust the time and location of your training.

- If a dog doesn't follow your treat as you lower it below her nose and move it slowly away from her, try pushing the treat slowly in and between her front legs instead of pulling it away from her body. As you push the treat in, watch the way the dog hunches her body. Go with the direction she hunches. If the dog's body slumps to the left or right, use the treat to keep facilitating that movement.

Once the dog has learned the mechanical motion of getting into the down position, add the sound "Down" immediately before your treat lure motion, and you're on your way. Just remember, as you practice:

- Cue "Down"

- Acknowledge "Good Boy"

- Treat within two seconds

- Release with "Okay"

- Get the dog up

Generalizing the Cue

Generalizing a cue means the dog understands that "Sit" means the same thing no matter where or when you give the cue. To achieve that, you'll need to practice the cue in a variety of situations so he will learn that no matter where he is cued, it always has the same meaning. By doing this, you avoid having to say to your dog trainer, "He always does it at home so I don't know why he won't do it here."

Practice cues in 10-minute sessions. Start in the quietest room in your home. Practice both sits and downs. Move the dog each time you give the cue. The sequence should be: "Sit," "Good Boy," treat, "Okay," move to a different location in the room. Next, you might do a "Down," "Good Boy," treat, "Okay," move to a different location in the room. Next you might choose to do "Sit," "Good Boy," "Down," "Good Boy," treat, "Okay," and move to a different location in the room.

After you have worked all around the quiet room, move to a different room and then a different room. Each time you practice, move to a room with more distractions. After you have practiced in all the rooms in your house, try the basement, the garage, the driveway, the yard, the sidewalk, then the local park. Then be creative. The more places you practice with your dog, the better he will understand that the cue always means the same thing, no matter where he is or what else is going on.

For the first 20 to 50 times you practice the cue, be sure to use "Good Boy" followed by the treat. This helps implant the cue in the dog's mind and it also helps establish your voice saying "Good-Boy" as a secondary reinforcer. After

50 to 100 repetitions with the food treat, you can move to random treats following your "Good Boy."

Proximity

How close the dog is to you may determine how well he pays attention. Assuming you are following my suggestions for creating structure and dealing with inappropriate behavior, and assuming you are using positive reinforcement rather than punishment as your preferred training method, you're likely to find that the closer your dog is to you, the better your control will be—at least in the beginning.

Use this knowledge as you train your dog. At first, teach your dog to do cued positions close to you. Don't be in a big hurry to see how far away you can get from your dog until he is rock solid on cues. Proof him by staying close, moving around him, even sitting down and standing up to see if he holds the cue. Next, in gradual increments, have adults, kids and other dogs walk past him as he holds the cue.

When he can handle distractions like these, cue the dog and start moving away from him in small increments. Invent distractions, test your dog. As he becomes solid at four feet away, add another foot. Keep testing. When you reach a distance the dog can't handle, go back to a distance where he is solid and spend some more time before adding more distance.

With this approach, you are in a position to reinforce your dog for good performance rather than constantly having to replace or correct him for moving before the release.

Section 15. Dogs on Leash

Leash Signals

Leash control is important to most of us because there are fewer and fewer places where it is safe to allow your dog to accompany you off leash. The leash is your signaling device to your dog. When your dog feels a change in the leash, it sends a message.

At first, a dog's reaction to leash pressure is clumsy. An uneducated dog bobs and weaves and runs out to the end of the leash. With your help, the dog learns that when she feels pressure coming from the leash, she must change what she is doing—slow down, change direction or back up. A wonder dog (what I call dogs who have it all figured out) feels every nuance from the leash. You could hold the leash with one finger, do an abrupt change of direction and the wonder dog will follow with no noticeable leash pressure.

Inappropriate use of the leash confuses your dog. She should never feel pressure when she is doing what you want. If she is sitting or lying beside you, the leash should be loose. If she is walking beside you, the leash should be loose. If you keep the leash tight all the time, your dog does not get the chance to make a mistake and learn from it. Every training procedure we give you is based on the premise that the dog's leash will be loose unless it is used to induce awkward pressure as a specific teaching strategy.

Puppies on Leash

When it comes to training, puppies are not much different

than dogs. They respond to positive reinforcement. They learn if things are presented to them clearly. The only difference that may hold you back is their level of socialization or life experience.

If a puppy has never experienced a leash, it may scare him until he knows what it's about. To orient a puppy to a leash, put a short line on the puppy and let him drag it around the house and yard (while under your watchful eye, of course). When the presence of the line is no longer an issue for him, make it a little longer. Then pick up the end of the line and follow the puppy around with no pressure on the line.

Once the line is no threat, begin to allow the puppy to experience what it is like to find the end of his line. To do this, just let him walk out to the end of the line. When he gets to the end, don't allow him to walk any farther. Just hold the line. He may pull against the end of the line. No matter what, don't let him move forward while pulling against the leash.

You can coax him back, make kissing sounds, call his name, offer him treats and just be patient. Eventually, the dog will stop pulling and look back at you. When he does, call him, coax him, squawk like a duck—get him to come back to you without pulling him. When he comes to you, give him a treat and praise him.

To begin teaching him to walk on a leash, follow the instructions below.

Leash Walking
Walking a dog on leash can be a nightmare. It's most

difficult for our older clients, for young children, and when the dog is an adolescent. Many people start the process by taking the dog for a walk. If things don't go well, some kind of walking aide is applied. It might be a slip collar (also known as a choke collar) or a pinch collar. The assumption is that the collar is designed to teach the dog to walk correctly. Usually the thinking is that if you put a slip collar on a dog, he will pull until the collar closes around his neck and then the choking will stop him from pulling. It doesn't work like that.

Unfortunately, taking a dog on a walk and teaching a dog to walk are two different things. It's like learning to read. You don't just hand your child a book and say, "Go to it." You start with learning letters, then sounds, then putting sounds together into words, then words into sentences, then paragraphs, then stories. Wow! Teaching a dog works the same way. We've got to teach the pieces and then put them together.

We start with one rule: **Never let the dog move forward while pulling.** If the dog gets to go forward while pulling, it's self-reinforcing.

From there you can find opinions galore. My approach is to start working with a flat collar to give the dog and owner some experience in attempting to walk without the dog pulling. If progress is not made, I move to power steering devices. My preferences include a walking harness, designed with the leash clip in front of the dog, on the chest by the breastplate. There are several companies that make these harnesses. If the walking harness doesn't work, I move to a snout collar or a head halter. Again, there are several types on the market. I find most dogs more easily accept the harness. If the dog does a lot of head throwing, tossing his head from side to side, lunging and the like, the head halter provides more control.

No matter what device the leash is connected to, we still want the dog's handler to learn some dog walking technique. The crux of the technique is to teach the dog that when she feels pressure on her leash or line, she needs to back off or change what she is doing. This takes patience and practice. It can seem very tedious to the dog handler. If you remember nothing else, you must refuse to allow any pulling to move the dog forward. This probably means planning your walks to be training sessions rather than your two-mile constitutional... at least until your dog gets in step.

Heeling is not necessary in the early stages of training a dog to walk. Heeling is a more precise activity that may come later. My walks begin with a general cue, "Let's Go." This signals the dog that we are on a mission and that there are rules. My process is outlined below.

Equipment
You need a leash or line long enough to allow a loose leash between human and dog. Where the leash hooks to the dog's collar, there should be a J shape as the leash drops down from the collar and then goes up to your hand.

Teaching the Leash Walk
Goal: The dog does not pull on leash.

Voice cue: "Let's Go" or "Come On"

Start your practice in a distraction-free environment. Orient the dog to the left side of the handler. The left side is the traditional dog walking side.

- Visualize a magic circle at your left side with a line through the middle of it emanating from your outside pants seam. The front edge of the circle should be the farthest point forward for your dog's head where he can still pay attention to you. Your magic circle should be big enough that the dog can walk in it without his head being so far forward that he can't keep track of you.

- Say "Let's Go," "Come On," or a cue of your choice. Use this cue every time you go for a walk. Be consistent.

- Use treats to create a hot spot for the dog at your outside pants seam. When the dog stays at your pants seam, treat liberally.

- Watch the dog's head. In a short time, you will begin to notice where the dog's head goes in reference to your magic circle and when he is no longer interested in you and is beginning a walk of his own.

- At the precise instant when the dog's head is signaling that he is on his own, change directions. Just go in the opposite direction. Keep the leash loose and signal your dog to come with you. You can use "Come On" or you can use the kissing sound. Encourage the dog to return to your side. When he does, treat, praise and keep walking.

- If your dog beats you—meaning you didn't respond quickly enough and he was able to run to the end of the leash—STOP immediately.

- Hold the leash still. Wait the dog out; no forward movement.

- Eventually, the dog will get tired of pulling and not being able to go anywhere. He will turn his head and look back at you. When he does, say "Good Boy," encourage the dog to move toward you and walk off in a new direction. When the dog catches up to your side, praise and treat.

- Another option when the dog runs to the end of the leash is to gently and slowly move backwards. This will more quickly encourage the dog to turn his head toward you. When he does, encourage him. When he catches up to your pants seam, praise and treat.

- Repeat the process I have just described.

- When you start actually walking in the real world, you may find that your dog walks nicely for part of the walk and tries to pull during another part. This allows you to use a flat neck collar for the easy part of the walk and then switch to the harness or head halter for the hard part.

- As the dog improves, try switching back and forth between the flat collar and the harness or halter, and pretending to switch back and forth, so the dog no longer pays attention to where the leash is hooked.

Dogs Off Leash

"My goal is for my dog to come when called when he is off-leash."

"I want my dog to stay in my yard without a leash or fence."

Each time I am presented with goals of this type, I respond by saying that I am extremely conservative when it comes to the safety of my dogs. Because of the way the world is today, I choose not to let my dogs off the leash unless I am sure I am in a secure area. Although I have several dogs who might be considered 95% reliable off leash, it is the other 5% of the time that can be the cause of their death. It's during that other 5% that they see the squirrel, rabbit or bird and decide to pursue. As an example of the devastation that can occur when this happens, here is the text of an e-mail received on an e-list we moderate.

Yesterday, my dog was hit by a car and killed. It's my fault. I let go of the leash for a split second to shut the door. He was lying down on the porch enjoying a bone.

He leaped up and ran out into the street. It's entirely my fault. I can't live with the guilt and the pain. It hurts too much just to force myself to breathe from minute to minute. He was the center of my life and my greatest love.

I have no coping mechanisms to deal with this loss, so I don't expect to survive it, but I wanted to take this opportunity to warn everyone: NEVER, EVER LET GO OF THE LEASH FOR A SPLIT SECOND.

Every dog owner I talked to yesterday has taken a million tiny risks, made a million little bad decisions that haven't ended in avoidable tragedy. I never thought it could happen to me either.

I worried obsessively about something happening to Dozer, but at the same time, it was surreal. I never believed, on some level, that it could happen.

Now my life will never be the same; I am permanently scarred and I don't know how I will get through today without him, let alone forever.

He is gone and it is all my fault. Don't let it happen to your dogs.

Moving Forward

From here, we up the ante. We have spent a few weeks working to establish a foundation structure and to build basic cues. Now we continue to expand the level of sophistication in your relationship with your dog.

Before you move forward, let's review what we have accomplished so far. We laid out a pre-training structure for life with your dog. We addressed some common questions asked by our clients. And we introduced basic cues. We also explained how to begin the fundamental training cues, including "Sit," "Down" and "Okay" (release), as well as walking on leash. If you have been practicing those things for about two weeks, 10 minutes per day for specific formal cues and 24-7 for in-home structure, you should be ready to move on.

If you have not yet spent time working on the skills and structure outlined previously, please don't move on. You can read ahead; just don't start working with the new material until the previous material is locked in. I ask this because your dog will have an easier time and experience less stress if the foundation is firm.

If you were a client at our facility, I would ask you the following questions before we proceed.

- Are you successful in ignoring, giving zero feedback to the dog when she offers undesirable behaviors that are not dangerous?

- Are you clear on who is part of your training program and who is not—meaning you must manage the dog in their presence?

- Is the dog solid on the symbolic feeding process? Does he sit and wait until released to get his food?

- Have you implemented the massage program? How is the dog doing?

- Do you have a clear position on what you expect from your dog in your home and with regard to getting on furniture and beds?

- Are you consistently using the sound "No" to mean "that's not what I want"?

- Are you consistently using the sound "Good Boy" to mean "you're doing the right thing and I like it"?

- Does your dog know the "Sit" cue and immediately put his rear on the ground when cued?

- Does your dog know the "Down" cue and immediately put his belly on the ground when cued?

- Does your dog understand the release cue and know that when he hears "Okay" he is free to move out of the position you previously cued?

- Have you generalized "Sit," "Down," "Okay," "No" and "Good Boy" to a variety of locations and situations?

If you are still having trouble with any of these areas, go back, reread the material about them and continue to work on them. Don't look at this as a pass-fail situation. It's simply a matter of how much time you have available and how difficult your dog is to work with. No one expects you to be a miracle worker. The fact that you are working through this at all puts you in a very special group of people.

If you're ready, we will now begin adding new activities to your repertoire.

Section 16. Attention and Recall

Attention Work

What I call attention work means getting the dog to focus on you—specifically, to look at your face on cue. Some people use cues such as "Look," "Look at Me," "Watch" or "Watch Me" for this. As always, I prefer a less artificial cue... something that seems to fit more easily into my day-to-day life with my dogs. Something I can use on the street without seeming odd or out of place.

My choice is to use the dog's name as a cue for attention. The process for teaching the name as an attention cue involves three steps. All three steps are conducted with your dog on a six-foot leash while you are comfortably seated in your evening chair, perhaps reading or watching your favorite television show or video.

Step One: Charge-Up

With six delicious treats in your hand or in a dish at your side:

- Say your dog's name and stick a treat in your dog's mouth as you say "Good Girl" or "Good Boy."

- The dog does not have to do anything except hear her name, eat the treat and hear you say "Good Girl."

- Getting the treat does not depend on the dog's behavior; it's the charge-up phase.

- If your dog is watching Animal Planet on television, reach around and put the treat in the dog's mouth.

- The dog hears your voice say her name, then, within a second or so, she hears your voice say "Good Girl" and is receiving a treat. She is learning to associate her name with the treat.

- This helps the dog begin to become more attentive when she hears her name—especially when she hears it said by your voice.

- On the first day, move immediately to step two.

Step Two: Turn-Look
With six treats in hand and your dog on leash:

- Wait until the dog turns her head away from you. When her head is turned, say the dog's name ONCE.

- When the dog turns toward you, say "Good Girl" and treat.

- When the dog again turns her head away, say her name ONCE.

- Wait till the dog turns and looks. Wait as long as it takes; if it takes half an hour, wait and say nothing.

- When the dog turns and looks, say "Good Girl" and treat.

- Repeat this process six times.

- On the first day, move immediately to step three.

Step Three: Final Focus
With six treats in your hand and the dog on leash:

- Wait until the dog turns her head. When her head is turned, say the dog's name ONCE.

- Wait until the dog turns toward you, then continue to wait until the dog either looks directly at your face or gives a quick eye flick to your face.

- The hard part here is to be patient until the dog gets around to looking at your face. You are trying to "catch" this behavior when it occurs and then reward it. The dog may look around, focus on other parts of your body, look at the treat, fidget, sit, lie down, etc., until she finally hits on the behavior that you want: a look at your face or an eye flick to your face.

- If the dog goes after the treat in your hand, close your fist around the treat and ignore her. She needs to learn that she never gets the reward by going after it, only by giving you what you want.

- When the dog looks at your face (direct look or eye flick), say "Good Girl" and give a treat. Don't be stingy here. If you think you see an eye flick, say "Good Girl" and give the treat. After a few times, the dog will start to get the idea that it is the face look you want and the eye flick will move toward a face look.

- Repeat this process six times.

Do all three steps the first day you start working on attention. The second day, drop step one, do a couple of step twos to get started, then move to step three. After the second day, use only step three. I suggest practicing step three six times every day to strengthen the cue.

Practice attention work until the dog looks at you expectantly when you say his name. This "charges" your dog's name to your voice and gets his focus on you. When the dog does a quick focus on you at the sound of his name, increase the distractions. Remember, **only say the dog's name once and use high-value treats.** If you add distractions and the dog doesn't respond, you have added too much too quickly. Go back to level where you had success and move forward more gradually.

To increase length of time the dog will focus on your face, continue to say "Good Boy" and treat, then pause and say "Good Boy" and treat again. Continue to repeat this sequence and wait longer between each "Good Boy" and treat. If you would like to put a release on this cue, say "Okay" and interrupt the dog's focus by moving.

I also recommend you become aware of how you are using the dog's name. Since we make the name more significant with this process, I suggest refraining from using the name unless it is significant. Instead, use other terms of endearment in routine daily communications, such as honey, beautiful, handsome, sweetheart or buddy.

The Recall

Recall means getting your dog to come back to you. Some people believe this should happen just because the human is the master and the dog is the dog. Many don't bother to think about what it is that would interest the dog in coming when he is called. For our discussion, I divide the recall into two categories: informal and formal.

Informal Recall

When you are hanging out with your dog in your backyard, at the park, at Grandma's house or even in your family room, and you call your dog saying, "Here girl, here buddy, come on sweetie," or the like, you are in what I think of as an informal recall situation. You have little control over the outcome. It's strictly up to the dog. She either comes or she doesn't; when she doesn't, it can be frustrating.

In the informal situation, your dog operates on her own motivational scale. I think of it as a 1 to 10 scale. You as the owner or handler are somewhere on that scale. Maybe you're an 8.5. If you're an 8.5 on your dog's scale and she is playing with a dandelion that is a 4.0, you win. The dog comes to you. If you call her and your Beagle is on the scent of a rabbit, which is a 9.5, you lose.

Your position on your dog's motivational scale can vary based on a variety of things. If you have been gone all day, you will be higher on the scale. If it's supper time for the dog and you call, you will be higher. If you've been with the dog all day, you may be lower. The bottom line is, the dog decides where you are on her motivation scale, and her response reflects your position.

Formal Recall

The other approach to recall is what I think of as a formal recall. It is heavily structured and it involves developing a conditioned response in the dog.

Training relationship: To help make this work, I suggest that you first establish a solid training relationship with your dog. Symbolic leadership activities, a positively reinforced cue structure (including clear voice tones), and clearly understood behavior parameters are part of this relationship.

Formal recall cue: The formal recall cue should not be used for anything else. So, for example, if you use "Come" for your informal cue, don't use it as a formal recall cue. The formal recall cue needs to be clear, simple and comfortable for you to say. Some options include: "Come," "Here," "Now" or "Front." You can teach the dog to come using any cue you want. Just keep it simple.

Training Sequence: Formal Recall

- Start by walking your dog on a six-foot leash. Let the dog wander away from you to the end of the six-foot leash (if your dog won't leave you, have someone distract him). Call the dog's name, followed by your formal recall cue (said distinctly). Then animate (cause excitement) as you move backwards away from the dog. The dog should chase you.

- As you move away, look for a spot where you can stop and the dog will end up landing in front of you in the sit position. Have a treat ready. Lure the dog to sit directly in front of you.

- The treats you use for the formal recall should be the best possible treats you can dream up. I often suggest this is the time to give your dog those bits of roast beef, chicken skin or cheese that you might otherwise withhold. In these exercises, always include a treat with your "Good Boy" as the dog hits the "Sit" in front of you. The randomness of treating in these exercises is what will the treat be, not whether there will be a treat. The idea here is for this cue to be perfect—so well-conditioned that the dog never considers anything else.

- Use the recall cue only once ("Spot, Come!"). Don't say "Sit" when the dog comes; instead, lure her into the sit position. Verbally praise the dog and give a high-value treat. Keep the dog sitting (use treats or leash and collar if needed). Release her with "Okay."

- Practice until the dog will return to you, sit in front and remain sitting without the need for excessive body language or coaxing.

Practice until the dog is proficient. My general rule is that the dog must be able to do nine of ten recall cues perfectly. He still must also do the tenth one, but it doesn't have to be perfect. It is not about how quickly you can get the dog off leash. The idea is that it does not even occur to the dog to skip or ignore the cue. Be 100% sure the dog will come to you. As the dog becomes reliable, add distractions.

- Once the dog is 100% reliable on a six-foot leash, with distractions, double the length of the leash by adding to it or use a long line. Repeat the process you used with the six-foot leash.

- Your energy level will make a difference in the dog's reaction. Use verbal and body language to encourage the dog to come to you. If the dog starts toward you, encourage with good girl, good girl, good girl, or pup, pup, pup, or kiss, kiss, kiss, kiss, and the like. Don't repeat the dog's name or the cue.

- If the dog starts toward you, encourage her. If the dog moves away or gets distracted, jiggle the leash, like a pager vibration, and say "No, No, No," until the dog turns back toward you. Then, encourage again with high energy. When the dog does nine of ten perfect with ten completions, double the length of the line again.

Continue the process I've described and continue doubling the length of the line until you have the dog as far away as you want to work with her. Once you are 10 or 12 foot away, I like parachute cord for the long line, because it's light but is 500-pound test. Light chord is less intrusive for the dog. If you like a handle, tie the chord to the end of the leash and use the leash for a handle.

- Next, work the dog off line in your house. If the dog ignores the cue and runs away from you, put him back on line. Do not let the dog rehearse skipping your formal recall cue.

- You can also play hide and seek with your dog in your house. Go hide; use the dog's name and the recall cue and expect the dog to find you. When she does, wait for the "Sit," praise, treat and release. If high-value treats are used, the dog is less likely to break away.

Practice until the dog is proficient. If the dog is not proficient, go back to an earlier step, increase the treat value and lower the distraction level. Never let the dog rehearse behavior you do not want.

As for sitting in front of whoever gave the recall cue, the dog should be close enough that the handler can reach down and comfortably grab the dog's collar where she is sitting.

When your dog is off leash, call only if you think she will come. If you don't think your dog will come to you, don't call her; go get her. And remember, your dog will not come to you if she experiences unpleasant consequences for coming. If she is always put away, taken in or, heaven forbid, scolded or beaten when she finally does come, you are making the recall worse.

Once he is doing well off line in the house, you can take him outside in a safe area (fenced backyard) and begin calling him to you and playing hide and seek around the yard with family members. Eventually you may want to call him from your house and give him his treat when he is sitting in front of you.

Finally, if at any time your dog is not coming to you when cued, he probably does not understand the cue in that particular context. Go back a step and work with him some more. Do not let the dog rehearse behavior you do not want.

Section 17. Solidifying "Sit" and "Down"

If you were successful in working with the "Sit" and "Down," you should be ready to begin increasing cue reliability. By successful, I mean your dog now clearly understands what body position to offer when he hears the "Sit" or "Down" cues, no matter where the cue is given, and he knows that when he hears the sound "Okay," he can move out of the cue and relax... as long as he maintains good manners. If your dog doesn't yet have these cues down solidly, it can be frustrating for him to move forward.

Up till now, I have not suggested working away from your dog. I have asked you to practice using the "Sit," "Down" and release cues in all kinds of circumstances with you close at hand. This is a process of conditioning the dog to the cue sound. Now we will expand the dog's expertise.

Duration
The act of remaining in position until released requires a different kind of learning from that of putting the body in a specific position when one hears a particular cue sound or sees a non-verbal signal. Duration is an entirely different concept. We will now begin to deal with that concept.

The Crossroads
We are now at a crossroads of sorts. Until now, we have suggested no activity that causes your dog even minor stress, unless you count stopping your dog from pulling and insisting that your dog sit to get her meals. As we move into developing duration in the "Sit" and "Down," I will

present two possible scenarios: one for those who believe a dog should never experience any discomfort of any kind under any circumstances and one for those who are willing to use what I describe as awkwardness to facilitate a faster learning curve.

As you read this, remember, this is a perfect example of "The map is not the territory." I mean reading about this process is different from actually doing it. If all the foundation stones are in place, this training should be no big deal for the dog. The only way you will know is to try it and watch the dog's reaction.

What Is Awkwardness?

Awkwardness occurs when the dog tries to go beyond the length of her leash or tether. It results from pressure the dog exerts against some part of her body (via collar, harness or head halter) as she pushes against a line or tether. Examples:

- **The dog forges ahead while on leash.** As she reaches the end of her leash, she creates pressure. The impact of that pressure depends on how fast the dog rushes to the end of her line. A good handler manages the situation so the dog has a limited space to move forward, therefore keeping the impact at the end of the leash soft. (We are assuming that the owner is not jerking the dog as she runs to the end of her line. The handler just prevents the dog from moving forward once the end of the line is reached.) The dog feels awkwardness as long as she continues to pull forward when the end of the line has been reached. As soon as the dog stops pulling, the pressure and the awkwardness go away. The handler then redirects, praises and rewards.

- **The dog is in a down position.** The handler has the ball of her foot on the dog's leash at a location that allows the dog full head and shoulder movement yet won't allow the dog to get into a full stand. The dog attempts to stand from the down position. The dog experiences awkwardness because he can not stand all the way up. As long as the dog continues to put pressure on the leash by attempting to stand, the awkwardness continues. Once the dog returns to the down position, the awkwardness goes away.

If proper foundation work has been done so the dog understands his cue and has practiced and been reinforced, this kind of awkwardness is very low on the stress scale and very short lived. If you don't find this to be true, go back and revisit your foundation work.

- **The dog is in a sit position.** The handler moves the leash so that it is up and between the dog's ears. The leash is loose and the dog has complete freedom of movement of head and shoulders. If the dog lifts his rear end off the floor, the handler applies *mild* pressure upward as the dog's rear lifts off the ground. Mild pressure is equivalent to that of a dress shirt and a tie on a human neck. For a dog, it's more an odd feeling than a stressful feeling. This awkwardness disappears as soon the dog's rear end starts back toward the ground. The pressure here is very mild—more a reminder to the dog that

something is out of kilter. The dog can move around,
even take a few steps with the awkwardness in place.

The key to this concept is that the awkwardness created by
pressure the dog generates against a leash or tether is
nothing more than a signal to the dog that something needs
to change. The handler does everything possible to assist
the dog in understanding what that something is. **There is
no jerking in this process.** The right body language, the
occasional lure, verbal encouragement—all these are used
to communicate how to get rid of the awkwardness. These
things, combined with good foundation work, make the
process simple and low stress.

Awkwardness is not used with a dog who is not ready. It is
the handler's responsibility to prepare the dog so that the
awkwardness will not be a frustrating experience. At our
facility, if a client has not done the required foundation
work, we will not use awkwardness with the dog. We have
no interest in frustrating the dog. This is a perfect example
of map and territory. Don't let your past programming
determine how you interpret this use of awkwardness.

Duration in the "Down" and "Sit"
Building duration in the down position begins with cueing
the dog to lie down, as you have been practicing. Once the
dog's belly hits the ground, acknowledge with "Good Girl"
and treat. Keep treating while you make sure the dog's
leash is laid out flat on the ground.

Now, put the ball of your foot on the leash at a point that
does not put any pressure on the dog. Be sure the dog's
head, neck and shoulders can move in all directions. If the

dog is pinned or has pressure from the line, her learning is hampered. The spot where your foot is on the line should also fix the line to be short enough that the dog can't get into a full stand.

- So far, no awkwardness exists for the dog as long as she remains in the down position. Keep feeding the dog small treats while she is in the down position. When the dog and you are comfortable, stop feeding treats. At first, stay by your dog for a few minutes. If she stays down, praise and treat. Next, try standing up or move back a step from the dog. If the dog stays down, acknowledge with "Good Girl," treat, "Good Girl," treat, with varying intervals between each pairing of "Good Girl" and treat.

- Keep adding more time between sequences of "Good Girl" and treat. Eventually, when the interval between acknowledgment and treat is long enough or the right distraction occurs, the dog will get up. When she does, she will quickly feel an awkward pressure as the leash stops her progress. When that happens, you say "No, Down" and wait. No leaning over the dog, no pushing on the dog, no stern voice, no pointing at the floor. Preferably no talking at all; just let the dog process what is going on.

- If the dog immediately begins to struggle, something is wrong. Either your preparatory work is not yet done or there is another problem. If you think it's the prep work, immediately lure the dog back into the down position and release with "Okay," then go back and continue working as described earlier, without the pressure. If you think it is something else, it's time to get help from a trainer or a behavior professional.

- Many times, if you have practiced the work outlined earlier, the dog will calmly lie back down. If so, acknowledge and treat. Then move away or stand up and relax. If the dog stands again, repeat the same sequence. Be patient; allow the dog to learn without pressure from you. The awkwardness here is no different than that used to stop the dog when she runs to the end of the leash.

In general, in all processes, I want the dog to learn that when she feels a change in leash pressure, she should change what she is doing and look for a different behavior that alleviates the awkwardness. A correct change releases pressure on the line. The handler then acknowledges and reinforces the desired change.

- If, when the dog stands up, she begins to look as if she doesn't have a clue what is going on or she becomes agitated because of the awkwardness of the leash, show her your treat (put it under her nose) and then move it to the ground and tap the ground in front of her. Say nothing. Keep tapping the ground. She may nuzzle the treat. Keep tapping the ground and say nothing. She will lie back down. When she does, acknowledge and treat.

- If done correctly, the dog may experience what looks like a bit of bewilderment when she stands the first time and feels the awkwardness of the leash. As the dog processes what is going on—without your involvement—she may show the beginnings of a little frustration. Don't give in too quickly; let the dog process the information. When you think the dog has had enough time to think it through and yet has not lain back down, hold the treat to her nose and then move it down and tap the floor again.

- When the dog lies down, acknowledge and treat. Stand back up, periodically tell the dog "Good Girl," and every few "Good Girls," add a treat. Space the treats out farther and farther as the dog figures out the game. Be careful not to treat too quickly after the dog gets up and goes back down, because you don't want her to think it's a jump up, drop down game. She should get the treat when she has been in the down position at least a few seconds... long enough to know that it is the "Down" you are reinforcing.

From here, you should set goals for your dog. Start with a goal of 15 or 30 seconds. You want the dog to be a winner, so don't set goals she can't meet. Your experience with your dog should guide you to the appropriate length of time for a down. When the dog reaches the 15- or 30-second goal, release her with "Okay" and make a fuss. Once that first goal is easy, add another 15 seconds. When she gets that one, add another 15 seconds. When you get to a minute, you can probably add 30-second increments. After the dog gets to three to five minutes, you may be able to add one-minute increments.

The important thing is that the dog wins every time. If she is fighting with you about staying down, your foundation work is not yet in place, you're trying to progress too fast, or there are too many distractions. Your dog *will* get this. Relax; it's about getting it done, not how fast you get it done. You want to accomplish the task and you also want to keep your relationship intact. When your dog starts accomplishing your goals, the sky is really the limit. You can keep adding to the goal until your dog can hold a 30- to 60-minute down if you wish.

One thing I ask is that you don't get into the "let's see how long we can keep her down" thing. When you do that, the dog has to lose because the only way you know how long she can stay down is to wait until she gets up. I'd prefer that you set goals you know are attainable. If you keep your focus on your dog as you go along, you will have a good sense of what your dog can do and how fast she can progress.

After a while, the awkwardness of the leash will be only a reminder to the dog. He will immediately return to the down position as soon as he feels the slightest sensation from the leash. Later, the reminder will not be needed.
We have noticed that the down is the easiest position for both dog and handler to get an understanding of duration when using this approach. After about a week, with daily practice, the dog seems to get a handle on how awkwardness relates to duration. After about a week of working on the down position using this procedure, it can be applied it to the sit position and the dog gets it quickly. Steps for the sit position follow. You will notice they are similar to those for the down.

Building duration in the sit position begins with cueing the dog to "Sit" as you have been practicing. When the dog's rear end hits the ground, acknowledge with "Good Boy" and treat. Keep treating while you arrange the leash so it goes up between the dog's ears to your hand. Be sure the dog's head, neck and shoulders can move in all directions. If the dog has pressure from the leash, his learning is hampered.

- So far, no awkwardness exists for the dog as long as he remains in the sit position. Keep feeding the dog small treats while he remains in the sit position. When the dog and you are comfortable, stop offering treats. Stay by your dog. If he remains in the sit position, praise and treat.

- Next, try moving one step back from the dog. If he remains sitting, acknowledge with "Good Boy," treat, "Good Boy," treat, with varying intervals between each pairing of "Good Boy" and the treat.

Keep adding more time between sequences of "Good Boy" and the treat. Eventually, when the interval between acknowledgment and treat is long enough, or the right distraction occurs, the dog will get up. When he does, quickly and smoothly (no jerking) put light, awkward pressure straight up on the leash. At the same time, say "No, Sit" and wait. No leaning over the dog, no pushing on the dog, no stern voice, no pointing. Preferably, no talking. Just let the dog process what is going on.

- If the dog begins immediately to struggle, something is wrong. Either your preparatory work is not yet done or there is another problem. If you think it's the prep work, lure the dog back into the sit position and release with "Okay," then go back and continue working on the cue without the leash pressure. If you think it is something other than the need for more practice, it's time to get help from a trainer or a behavior professional.

- Many times, if the work outlined earlier has been practiced, the dog will calmly sit. If so, acknowledge and treat. Then move away to a distance that is successful for the dog and relax. If the dog stands again, repeat the same sequence. Be patient; allow the dog to learn without pressure from you.

In general, in all processes, I want the dog to learn that when he feels a change in leash pressure, he should change what he is doing and look for a different behavior that releases the awkwardness. A correct change releases pressure on the line. You then acknowledge and reinforce the desired change.

- If, when the dog stands up, he begins to look as if he doesn't have a clue what is going on or he becomes agitated because of the awkwardness of the leash, show him your treat, put it over his nose and then move it back toward his rear end. When he sits back down, acknowledge and treat.

- If the dog continues standing, be patient and use your treat and hand motion. Don't give in too quickly; let the dog process what is going on. When you think the dog has had enough time to think it through, if he has not returned to the "Sit," put the treat to his nose and move your hand toward the rear end again.

- When the dog sits, acknowledge and treat. Periodically tell him "Good Boy," and every few times, add a treat. Space the treats out farther and farther as the dog figures out the game.

From here, you should set goals for your dog. Start with a goal of 15 or 30 seconds. You want the dog to be a winner, so don't set goals he can't reach. Your experience with your dog should guide you to the appropriate length of time for a "Sit" goal. When the dog reaches the 15- or 30-second goal, release him with "Okay" and make a fuss. When that first goal is easy to reach, add another 15 seconds. When he gets that one, add another 15 seconds. When you get to a minute, you can probably add 30-second increments to your goal. A one- or two-minute "Sit" is a good goal.

- The important thing is that the dog wins every time. If he is fighting with you about staying in the sit position, your foundation work is not yet in place, you're trying to progress too fast, or there are to many distractions. Your dog *will* get this. Relax; it's about getting it done, not how fast you get it done. You want to accomplish the task and you also want to keep your relationship intact.

After a while, even the slightest awkwardness will be a reminder to the dog and he will immediately return to the sit position—probably faster than you can say anything. Eventually, he will not even need the reminder.

No Awkwardness

For those who feel that the use of awkwardness as I've described is too much for your dog, you can accomplish the same end result using the same process but eliminating the use of the leash to provide awkwardness when the dog gets up.

Every time your dog gets up without being released, say "No," repeat the cue, replace the dog and reward. Use your "Good Girl," treat sequence to acknowledge the dog and reinforce. Keep realistic goals. If the dog is getting up frequently, your goals may be too much for her.

Without the awkwardness, it may take you more time to build duration and your dog may be less reliable in maintaining the position until released. Keep working and keep your goals and distractions realistic.

The caution here is not to reward your dog for getting up. This can happen if she gets up, you lure her back down and give her a treat immediately. If she does this repetitively, she may think the game is stand up, lie down, get food. To curb this, be sure the dog is in a sit or down position for a few seconds before giving the treat. In other words, make sure the dog knows the treat is coming for duration, not for jump up, lie down.

Nonverbal Hand and Body Signals as Cues

Signals of any kind, used consistently and with clarity, can be used to let the dog know what we want. When a dog looks at us, she sees everything about us. What we must do is present ourselves in such a way that the dog can tell what she is supposed to pay attention to and what she can ignore or screen out.

A dog can pick up on a motion, even a small one, and learn that it signals an action. But dogs can have difficulty decoding the message we are trying to send if we are making too many movements or our movements are inconsistent. Our job is to decide what signals we want to use and make them clear and consistent. Just about any signal will do, as long as the dog can pick it out. I have a friend who does all his nonverbal signals with his fingers. The movements are minimal yet very precise. His dog watches him like a hawk and performs perfectly.

Typical nonverbal signals involve movement of the arms and hands. They could be done with any part of your body that the dog can discriminate. My typical signals are:

- **"Come"**: An arm swing toward my chest, starting with my arm straight out to my side at shoulder height. My hand is open and at the end of the signal my palm ends up on my chest. The arm swing is motioning the dog toward me.

- **"Down"**: An arm swing down from the elbow, starting with my arm bent 90 degrees and my hand at shoulder height. At the end of the signal my palm is open and facing the ground. The trick here is for the

196

dog to see the palm of the hand moving downward. If the dog is 100 yards away, my arm movement may begin high above my head. If my dog is at my side, only the palm of my open hand with little movement may be enough.

- **"Sit"**: I begin with my elbow close to my body and my arm straight out in the front of the body. My hand rolls over, moving to palm up as the stroke ends. The arm rolls just slightly as the hand is turned over. The closer the dog is to me, the smaller the roll of the arm. For a great distance, the roll over of the hand should be more exaggerated.

None of my signals are magical. Don't worry if you have trouble deciphering my directions. Remember, any signal you invent and use clearly and consistently will work. You could bow your head for "Down," lift your left leg for "Sit" and bow at the waist for "Come," if that's what you like. Remember my friend who uses his fingers to signal.

Teaching Nonverbal Signals

When you use a lure to teach the "Sit," "Down" and recall, that motion can establish a foundation for nonverbal signals. Think back to when you used a treat to move the dog's head back so he put his rear on the floor or placed a food ball under the dog's nose to lure him to the ground. Those motions may already be in the dog's mind. If so, those motions may help if your nonverbal signals are done with your arms and hands.

Even if you are starting from scratch, as long as your dog is responding reliably to your verbal "Sit," "Down" and "Come" cues, you can add a nonverbal cue. Here is how it's done:

- Perform your nonverbal signal and then immediately (within seconds) say your verbal cue.

- When the dog performs the cued action, acknowledge and reward. Release before the dog gets up on her own.

- Continue using this sequence until you notice your dog beginning to move into the cued position before the beginning of your verbal cue. Withhold your verbal cue a little longer after you give your nonverbal cue to test the dog's understanding.

- When the dog seems to understand the nonverbal cue, try using it without the verbal cue. If the dog performs the cued action, the nonverbal cue is in place.

- From that point, practice verbal cues only, nonverbal only, and both verbal and nonverbal together. If the dog's performance drops off, go back to the first step in this sequence and start again. The dog will regroup quickly.

You can use a nonverbal cue for any action you can teach. The only criterion is that the dog must be able to see the cue. Always remember that you reinforce and release an action cued with a nonverbal cue just as you do with a verbal cue.

Section 18. Home Base and Time Out

A Portable Home Base

"Place," "Perch," "Bed," "Carpet," whatever you want to call it, teaching your dog to find and stay with a portable station of some type is a good practice. This cue can be taught at any time during your foundation building. I usually start after the dog has a working knowledge of "Good Boy," "No," "Sit" and "Down." This is only because these cues are fundamental in my model and the process dogs experience while accomplishing them makes learning other things easier, including "Place."

I suggest using a small rug, mat, towel, carpet or other easy-to-clean material as home base—the "place" you send your dog. I like something washable. It also helps if the material lies flat without wrinkling. Your mat should be easy to carry. You can move it from room to room, to Grandma's house, to the facility where you train the dog. No matter where it is, it provides a comfortable spot with a familiar scent for your dog.

Defining the Cue

Teaching your dog to go to "Place" begins with a definition of the cue. "Place" can mean "go to your mat and lie down or sit." It can also have a more general meaning, such as "keep any appendage on the mat and you are in compliance." A tail or foot on the edge of the mat can qualify as contact. I have had dogs who will walk around the edge of the mat, lie down with one foot on the mat and never lose mat contact. You've got to define what behavior

200

you want because that is what you are going to reinforce.

Suppose your definition will be go to the mat and keep some part of the body on it. With that definition to start, you will be reinforcing your dog when he hits the mat with any part of his body, often his foot.

Steps to Home Base

- Begin by getting your dog's attention and then throw the mat on the floor so your dog can see it.

- Show your dog a treat and use some body language pointing to the mat as you toss the treat on the mat. When the dog goes to the mat to get the treat, praise with "Good Boy." Continue dropping treats on the mat to keep the dog on it.

- Release with "Okay" and move the dog off the mat before he walks off on his own.

- Repeat tossing treats. Praise the dog when he steps on the mat, release and move the dog off the mat.

- When the dog easily follows the treat to the mat, add the cue "Place" or what ever cue you like. Say the cue just *before* you toss the treat onto the mat. Motion toward the mat, wait for the dog to step on the mat, then praise with "Good Boy," treat, release and move the dog off the mat.

- If the dog moves off the mat before he is released, say "No" (that's not what I want), guide the dog back onto the mat, praise with "Good Boy," treat, and when you are ready, release and move the dog off the mat.

- Initially, your release should be based on observing the dog. Use praise and reinforcement to encourage the dog to stay on the mat. When you have squeezed out as much time as you can get, release the dog and move him off the mat.

- Set goals as you did when developing duration for the "Sit" and "Down" cues.

- Be very consistent! When you ask, be sure your dog accomplishes the cue. Be sure you release him. If the dog moves off before your release, place the dog back on the mat, praise and reward.

- Repeat the previous steps from all angles of approach to the mat, then increase the distance from the mat.

- Finally, move the mat to different positions, rooms and geographic locations to generalize the cue and the "Place" action.

If the process is not working, it's likely you are moving too fast or you are not being consistent. Go back and restart the process at a level where the dog can be successful. Ultimately, this process can be used as a home base for your dog for unlimited amounts of time at any location.

Time Out

Everyone has their own idea about time out, what it is, how to use it, even if it should be used at all. Our experience has been that time out can be effective when used in a specific context. What you will notice is that our approach to time out is very structured. If you just arbitrarily put the dog away when she does something you don't like, it's very confusing to the dog. For time out to be effective, the dog must be able to connect a specific behavior with her time out. For example, it might be jumping on guests when they arrive at the door. Here is the framework we use.

- With time out, work on changing just one behavior at a time. Decide what that behavior will be.

- Pick a cue to mark the behavior you are working to change. I prefer short, simple cues, such as "Too Bad," "That's It" or "It's Over."

- Every time the dog does the behavior, mark it once with the cue.

- Immediately after marking the behavior with the cue sound, take the dog unceremoniously to her time out spot. Be as bland and uncommunicative as you can; no conversation, no lectures, just directly to time out.

- The time out spot should be away from the party. For me, the party is where the dog wants to be. If she wants to be at the door, her time out spot should be in a different room where she can't see, hear or relate to the party.

- A crate can be used for time out. That does not make the crate a bad thing. The discomfort for the dog is being removed from the party. How the dog relates to the crate will be determined by how the crate is normally used with the dog.

Our dogs are in crates at night and at other times when we or they need a break. Our dogs are always given treats when they're in their crates—except when they are in a time out. You can also use a safe room for time out. A safe room could be a laundry room, garage, basement or bathroom—any room where your dog has little entertainment and can't get into trouble.

- The dog remains in time out for a minimum of three to five minutes. The dog must be quiet and calm for the last three minutes she is in time out.

- If it takes the dog 20 minutes to calm down, the full time out would be 23 minutes. Don't worry, it doesn't usually take the dog long to learn that she does not get out unless she is quiet.

- Never go to a dog when she is making a fuss. It teaches her that making a fuss will get her out of the time out. We want her to learn that being quiet gets her out of the time out.

- Obviously, don't put your dog in a crate if you think she will do damage to herself. If this is likely, you should be working with a certified trainer or behavior professional.

Remember my rules for good behavior: sitting, standing or lying down and not vocalizing. My dogs don't get out of the time out until they meet that standard. It's all about clarity with the dog. My dogs get ignored if they are making a fuss. My procedure for ignoring was explained in Section 13.

One of our dedicated clients rescued a Boxer. His wife told me that after beginning our training process, he actually waited two hours for the dog to settle down before he let her out of her crate. That's dedication. And that's what is sometimes necessary if a dog has been previously reinforced for an unwanted behavior. These unwanted behaviors are often unknowingly reinforced by owners who don't understand how the process works. When a dog is rescued, we often don't know the dog's background. In many cases, unbeknownst to their new owners, rescue dogs have been reinforced for undesirable behaviors.

- When the dog has been quiet for three minutes, I put her on a leash and take her out of the crate or safe room and back to the party. If the dog does the unwanted behavior again, I instantly mark it with "Too Bad" and again, unceremoniously take her back to time out (away from the party).

- Repeat this process as many times as you can stand it in a given setting. If you reach a point when you don't want to try again, leave the dog in the time out until the visitor is gone.

- The one thing you do not do is give in. You can repeat the process as many times as you can stand it, and you don't ever let the dog in to the party when she does the behavior you are working on.

- The dog needs to learn that every time she starts to lift her feet to start a jump, she hears your cue, "Too Bad," and she ends up out of the party.

- When the dog can enter the room and keep her feet on the ground, she gets to stay at the party.

- When jumping is the problem, you can help the dog be a winner by having her on a leash when a visitor comes to the house so you can immediately react to her behavior.

- When introducing the dog to a visitor, if it is safe, have the visitor offer a treat in an open hand at her side so the dog's focus is low and she is less likely to jump.

- You can also do this when your visitors have moved to your living area and are seated when you bring the dog in.

- Again, keep the dog on leash while she is learning. That way, you can immediately mark the undesired behavior and move the dog to time out.

Don't use time out for more than one behavior at a time. It could confuse the dog. Clarity and simplicity are the keys here. The cue must be clear and immediately connected with the behavior in question. The move to time out is quick, without punishment or other interaction; just very matter-of-fact. Remember: clear, quick, simple—that's what makes it work.

Time out is just one strategy for your tool box. As you go through this book, you should be coming to understand that these principles, combined with your creativity and planning, offer many options for working with your dog.

Section 19. Problem Solving

Once your basics are in place, you are in a position to solve problems. The process used when we help a client solve a problem with their dog is the same as used by many counselors when they help humans solve human problems.

Behaviors vs. Labels

One of the first things we need to do to solve a problem is carefully define it. To do this requires some knowledge about the difference between behavior and labels. Labels are generalized statements we make that may not be helpful in problem solving; behaviors are specific and observable. For a human, being called **lazy is a label; not reporting to work on time is a behavior.** When applied to dogs, here are general statements we frequently hear:

- My dog totally freaks out all the time.

- My dog never stops barking.

- My dog tears the house up every time I leave.

- My dog has destroyed my whole house.

- My dog is aggressive.

- My dog attacks strangers.

- My dog hates my spouse.

- My dog loves children.

- My dog doesn't listen.

- My dog is not aggressive, just protective.

- My dog loves everyone.

- My dog is jealous.

- My dog never stops jumping.

- My dog won't eat.

- My dog loves me.

- My dog understands what I say, I know it.

A more helpful statement is an observable description of the dog's behavior. Here are some examples:

- My dog jumps back, barks and runs around in circles for five minutes every time I let someone in my front door.

- My dog barks when I tie him to the tree behind the house.

- When I go to work, I leave the dog loose in my apartment. When I come home, the waste basket is turned over and papers are torn and scattered across the kitchen.

- When I let a stranger in my front door, my dog stands beside me and barks and shows his teeth.

- When I come home from work, my dog jumps up on me and licks my face.

- When my dog is outside in the fenced backyard and I call him, he continues to sniff the ground.

Problem analysis requires a fresh look to clarify the nature and magnitude of the problem, as well as to establish how the problem will be resolved and by whom. As circumstances become more complex or sensitive, problems can become nightmares if a clear method for analysis is not available.

The approach for clearly identifying a problem and determining the appropriate person to deal with it either moves the problem to an efficient resolution or mucks up the water. When I work with a client, I guide him through a specific process. When we come back together after the dog owner has had some time to work on a problem, I go back through the process to see what has worked and what has not. We then rework the process as required to get our desired end.

You can use the process yourself to work through problems you feel capable of tackling. Involve everyone who would be involved in making the plan work. If you run into trouble, get the help of a certified trainer or behavior professional.

Solving Problems

Once you know how to clearly identify your problem, we apply the following problem-solving process. The problem-solving process itself is very basic. The steps you'll use in problem solving and planning are:

1. Define the problem.

2. Identify criteria or expectations that must be met.

3. Brainstorm possible solutions.

4. Evaluate solutions.

5. Choose the best solution for your current circumstances.

6. Make a detailed plan.

7. Set up a process for reviewing the progress of that plan.

8. Recycle and revise the plan as circumstances require.

Define

Clear definition of the problem or problems is the most critical step in getting an appropriate solution.

First you must do the preliminary training work I have

already outlined throughout this book. If that has been determined to be too dangerous, you should be working with a certified professional.

With the ground work in place, you move to problem solving. If there are 10 problems, you must prioritize them and deal with each one individually. It's like eating an elephant: You've got to do it one bite at a time.

Here is where you must describe the dog's issues in terms of observable behaviors. The more details the better. For example, when someone knocks on the front door, the dog immediately runs to the door and stands there barking. After the visitor is let in, the dog runs under the end table by the couch and continues barking. When you holler "No" to get him to stop, it does no good. After about 20 minutes, the dog stops barking and goes to the corner by the piano and lies down.

Expectations

Identify what factors must exist or what requirements must be met for a solution or plan to be successful. Here are some examples of general criteria. You can add specific criteria that fit your circumstances.

- Is the solution efficient as opposed to other alternatives?

- Is it workable in practical application?

- Does it generate bigger problems?

- Does it fit in with my values?

- Is it fair to the dog?

- Can all who must be involved accept the solution?

Brainstorm

Use the brainstorming process to identify possible solutions. Remember, even though it sometimes appears as if there is only one path available, **there is always more than one option.** Sometimes just a small variation in an idea or combining elements from several ideas ends up as the best available option.

In the brainstorming process, the goal is to come up with the maximum number of possible solutions. To accomplish this, consider anything. Don't rule out any suggestion, no matter how far out it may sound at first. This guideline is critical to making the concept work.

To make this process most effective, it may be valuable to take a break after brainstorming is done. After reflection, even more ideas may pop up to be added to the list.

- When searching for possible ideas, search the Internet, too. There are many organizations that offer ideas to help solve problems.

- As you search, remember any potential solution must fit your value system. If you have read this book through, you know what that means.

- Above all, remember, do no harm.

Evaluate
Examine the pluses and minuses of each idea generated. Evaluate based on the available data as well as your opinions.

Choose
In this step, the best solution rises to the top of the pile and is formally chosen as a course of action. If it's a family affair, consensus is usually the best choice. Be cautious about moving to a quick vote that creates winners and losers. Those who lose often have resentment that works against desired goals.

Consensus itself is on a continuum. Even those who will support a decision may not be thrilled about doing so. Be sure that every person who has a responsibility for the solution has specifically agreed that he or she will do it.

Plan
Undertake the critical process of devising a carefully thought-out implementation plan. That's when the focus turns to the who, what, when, where and how of the solution. Be sure each step of each solution is spelled out so everyone understands. Renew the commitment of each person who has a responsibility in the plan.

Review
Recognize that you don't have to find a solution that lasts forever. Sometimes you start with a temporary fix knowing that later you will be able to do better. Knowing this, build

in a follow-up discussion for evaluating the solution and determining what's next.

Recycle

The process is recycled any time the plan runs into trouble and as many times as necessary to deal with the issue at hand. Remember that a glitch in the plan is nothing more than a new or unforeseen problem that needs to be solved. Don't get discouraged. If it seems overwhelming or if you can't seem to find good options, get help.

The problem-solving process I have presented is fairly rational and structured. It gives you a conscious model for working through your problems and being sure all bases are covered. From here, and to complete this book, I will offer some thoughts about how our intuition may influence our work with dog behavior and training.

When working with a dog who has complex behavior problems or who is in a complex environment, a path to resolution isn't always clear. In these situations, I find myself engaged with, sometimes consumed by, the problem all my waking hours. Sometimes my waking hours are increased because of these kinds of problems. When this happens, I am very much aware that my intuition is at work. The next section will give you some insight into my perception of how intuition helps us when working with our dogs.

Section 20. Intuition

When planning and solving problems, some people believe strongly in their intuition while others believe they are completely rational, operating only from facts, and refuse to consider that intuition plays any part in their decision-making. If you hold the latter belief, the question for you is, What mechanism do you use to evaluate those facts and how large a role does it play?

A Rational Basis
We often hear of rational processes (like that in the previous section) for problem solving. Yet, when all is said and done, something within us says, This is what makes sense. This is what adds up. This is intuition, and it's at its strongest when hard science is scant, incomplete or inconclusive.

Even solid science has a subjective element. This is borne out in the scientific community with the acknowledgement that it is difficult to keep any experiment entirely pure. The reason is that the experimenter is thought to have an effect on the results of the experiment. This may show up in the way the experimenter chooses to set up, observe and evaluate during an experiment. These factors, combined with a personal bias (or hope) about what might happen, can make a difference in how the results of the experiment are interpreted.

Intuition and Reality
If positions taken by human beings are, in part, based on

intuition, then what our intuition tells us becomes even more significant. If, as some believe, our intuition taps into what others say and do as we talk to them, listen, conduct surveys—all seemingly concrete activities—or by other, less definable means, then intuition has an impact on practical reality. Intuition tips us off about when to back off, when to provide support, what decisions make sense, as well as how to apply what we know to influence others.

The Reliability of Intuition

The answer to the question, "Is intuition reliable?" is found in the success of our decisions. The criteria used to evaluate decisions is often related to how well decisions fit into what is acceptable for the people who will be affected by the decision.

From a practical standpoint, it's good to have maximum information available, on a conscious basis, while the intuition process is working in the background. Having a good grasp of relevant concrete information can help us be confident that no matter what role intuition plays, we are still on solid footing. Anything else is a bonus.

A Structure to Work With Intuition

Mastering the use of intuition is easier if we understand some working definitions. Working definitions imply that there is a stated meaning for certain words as they appear in a particular context.

Because the scientific methods available to clarify sources of intuition and evaluate its accuracy are in a state of infancy, differences of opinion exist. Listed below are some definitions that may be helpful in understanding intuition.

Intuition: Knowledge obtained without rational thought; innate or instinctive knowledge; immediate comprehension or cognition; "knowing that you know"; insight (seeing into a situation); discernment (ability to grasp what is obscure); realization that may arrive at a seemingly magical moment, possibly after a long pondering of the problem. Intuition can also be expressed as a hunch or gut feeling.

Conscious mind: The part of the mind that processes information, that is logical, organized, reasonable; focusing attention; perceiving or noticing with some controlled thought; aware (drawing inferences from one's experiences); the place where you think things through.

Subconscious: The place where things "gel," usually without our awareness. The place where information, opinion, facts, subtle signals and rote memorization of formulas, charts and actions, come together to yield the answer to a problem. This all happens without our being aware that the process is taking place. In a practical sense, it allows us to type on a keyboard without looking at the keys; it's "knowing" the answer to eight times eight; it allows us to play a musical instrument or to flawlessly execute a karate move under pressure.

Intention: Intention, as used with intuition, is a clarification of what you are looking for. In stating your intention, it seems to work best when formed as an answer sought or a problem to be resolved. However, you are not saying you want the problem solved in a specific way. You leave all options open so your intuitive process can explore a wide spectrum of opportunities. This is a different type of intention statement than when you state the intention to complete something in a specific way.

Open intention statement: When looking for problem resolution or direction, an example of an open intention statement might be something like this: "My intention is (or, I need) to find a solution to my dog's problem barking when I release him in my fenced yard." When you form an intention statement, use your own words and remember to keep it open so you don't restrict your intuition as it does its work. Evaluating what you get can come later.

Ignition point: Building a fire requires generating enough friction to produce the heat to ignite a fuel source. The more easily a fuel source bursts into flame, the less effort is required to produce ignition. An ignition point also exists with people in terms of their receptivity to ideas. In some situations, because of experiences they have had or the way they have been prepared, people are ready to receive and support certain ideas. The more information and experience we have concerning the problem we are working on, the more our intuition has to work with. A key here is to be open enough that unique or unusual ideas are allowed to form and be considered.

Something to think about: Thomas Edison was once asked where he got his ideas. His answer was that they are floating around in the air.

Where Intuition Takes Place

Conscious consideration is active thinking about a topic, issue or problem while being aware of doing so.

219

Subconscious processing happens without our awareness. Intuition can happen between conscious thoughts, in addition to conscious consideration and at times that seem to be totally separated from awareness of the topic or issue. Those times can include when you sleep, eat lunch or drive, as well as while being stimulated in other ways, such as off-topic conversations, watching a movie, listening to music, attending inspiring lectures or while exercising.

During these times we may have thought fragments, simple thoughts, streams of thoughts—entire plans or solutions may even arise. Whether a flash of intuition happens during a training session or on the drive home doesn't matter. Either can be helpful.

When your intuition is working, you have a strong sense that you "know" but you may not know how you know. The trick is not to tune out or intellectualize away these bits of knowing when they happen. Since intuitive bursts can fade quickly, it's best to write them down or somehow record them right away. It's impossible to know when intuitive thoughts will occur and they can slip away as fast as they come.

Often, these bursts of insight hold up under scrutiny during a discussion with our peers. Sometimes these bits of knowing don't prove to be the answer. Even those flashes that don't prove to be "the answer" can serve as a conduit that leads to a better decision. Occasionally, these "knowings" are completely shot down when scrutinized within a known zone of acceptance.

Enhancing Intuition

Focusing intuition requires only that the objective is clearly in focus and tucked into your mind while you go about your business, content that your intuition will work toward a solution. Answers or partial answers may come at any time: when falling asleep, in dreams, as you abruptly awake in the middle of the night or as first thoughts in the morning.

Intentional reflection requires that we determine an intention and then allow our mind to contemplate, even wander, for a result, without obvious distractions. Preferably, this is done in a quiet setting where people are unlikely to disturb you. Some people lean back in their chair. Others add soft music. Still others go to a favorite spot. Some like to hear birds singing, wind blowing, water rippling or waves crashing on a beach.
The secret is not to have an agenda. Allow your mind to work with no expectations about results or how and when they may show up. For some, awareness will occur during this time of reflection; for others it may show up at a later time, often when least expected... like on the drive home, while exercising or at a movie.

Prayer is another way to enhance intuition. With your intention clearly in mind, and according to your religious affiliation or spiritual beliefs, enter into a prayerful state and ask in the appropriate way for guidance that will allow you to best reach a solution. Again, answers may not be immediate.

Meditation is another possibility. There are various methods of meditation. Most are looking for a way to relax the body and clear the mind of distracting thoughts. This allows higher-level thinking to occur, often without conscious awareness.

The binaural beat was patented as a tool to induce brain wave patterns that help us reflect, think, relax and even increase creativity. Binaural beats are apparent sounds, the perception of which arises in the brain independent of physical stimuli. They are not recorded at a level that can be heard. These beats combine to create desired brain wave states.

The Monroe Institute of Faber, Virginia, is a pioneer in this science. Some formats for binaural beats include:

- **Natural sounds:** These involve the use of waves or other nature sounds. The listener just leans back and listens to the soothing sounds. The binaural beat is not noticeable.

- **Guided imagery:** Here, the beats are combined with soothing sounds and a voice to guide relaxation and focus direction. Again, the binaural beats cannot be heard. *The Essence of Wisdom* (available from the Monroe Institute) is one of my favorite audio guides for reflection. It uses a subtle verbal guide to ask if there are other ways a problem may be viewed.

- **Meta music:** This approach uses music as a vehicle for the binaural beats. Some selections combine with beats that help increase concentration. Others help with relaxation and encourage focus or creativity.

Music compositions also vary to fit personal taste. We have used *Inner Journey* (available at the Monroe Institute) as background music in our reactive dog classes. It helps calm both humans and dogs. We also like *Sleeping Through the Rain* and *Cloudscapes* for general relaxation.

Most Important

Trust that your intuition and creativity are at work. Don't set up expectations about what, how or when things should happen. No matter which approach you decide to use, follow your own path. If you choose to use guided imagery and the instructions become cumbersome, go with your own lead. Remember, you have been doing fine up until now.

Curb your expectations for startling blasts of revelation and relax while your intuition works for you. Pay attention to your environment and notice where you tend to get the best results. Is it when you are sitting, lying down, at the park, in the woods, on the lake, while jogging?

Results of the Intuitive Effort

Results may be subtle to dramatic. If the result of your chosen course provides you with a startling revelation, the process will seem valid. If it is subtle, even to the point where it seems nothing has occurred, the process is simply not over.

- You may be startled by a very concrete thought that says, "do this" (sometimes really big, sometimes not). This could include an unexplained feeling that you need to talk to a particular person or to browse a particular bookshelf. You might even find yourself with an urge to attend a particular seminar, where— low and behold—a speaker, maybe one you were not planning to hear, says something that provides just what you need.

- You may also find yourself befuddled because nothing clearly presents itself. The reality is that intuition will not be pressured. It won't be consciously manipulated. In some cases, it may take a form or present a message that you are not ready to acknowledge. You can do things that may encourage or support your intuitive process, but it is unlikely that it will perform on demand to yield a result you dictate.

It's not that your intuition has abandoned you. It's more likely that, because of your psychological state, you are "jamming" the intuitive message and it can't get through. The more you use your intuition, the easier it may be for you to recognize its messages, even under pressure.

A helpful thing to aid your intuition is to identify problems or situations early so that your intuition can work with less pressure, over time. Last-minute crises, dealt with under high stress, may not be the best time to say, "Intuition, don't fail me now."

If your intuitive response is subtle, if you can't find a clear message, it can be very frustrating. If this is your usual result, you may even want to discount the whole idea as fruitless. If this happens, don't give up. Remember, intuition most often gives you pieces or directs you to the next step. If you work with others, they may help you firm up ideas as you hear their insights. In fact, the reflections and discussions of a group may provide the ignition point that solidifies your intuition into an idea that may be acted upon.

- If you are on your own and not part of a group and your reflection yields unclear results, don't be discouraged. Just keep your intention focused on what you need to know and go about your daily affairs. While you do this, your intuition continues to percolate on the problem.

- This percolation can last for hours, days, weeks, months, even years (Yes, years. Think about those sudden unexpected insights about career changes or finding that perfect partner). This is why it's important to identify problems and goals early, to allow as much time as possible to plan.

- You must trust that your conscious and unconscious mind have the capacity to work the problem out, to move you to the next level, or to point to the place where you need to go for help. You may even find part of your answer in a television program or a radio broadcast that you casually seek out.

Complementing Intuition

Help often centers on seeking people whose wisdom is respected and asking them open-ended questions. Once a question is asked, the goal is to listen—not the type of listening that focuses on what to say next, but rather, the kind that seeks all the meaning possible.

- This also includes resisting the temptation to engage in dialogue until your source has offered all the information available.

- Once sources of wisdom have been consulted and their input is combined with other available information and data, ideas may begin to solidify. Often they yield more than one option or path.

You can never be sure when the intuition process is finished. If you discover that your ideas are out of sync with those you are working with, both dog and human, being open enables you to consider modifying your ideas. Remember, one of your jobs is to find a direction that will fit into the zone of acceptance that exists because of the belief systems of those involved.

In "The Zone"

Being in "The Zone" (as differentiated from the zone of acceptance) is a concept that's often discussed with regard to firing-line performance. This type of performance may be seen at an athletic event when a player makes just the right move at the precisely the right time. It may also be seen when high-stress or critical moments present the need for rapid-fire decisions to fix a problem or avoid a crisis. In our dog behavior work, this kind of thinking often shows up in our Reactive Dog classes.

In situations like these, there may appear to be no conscious thought; just action. In other situations, several options may seem to appear from nowhere, in rapid-fire succession. In these cases, conscious thought may occur as a choice is made among the options. Sometimes an outside opinion is quickly sought as the ultimate choice is considered. Other times the whole process is handled internally.

This form of being in "The Zone" is based on all that has come before: your skills, your homework, as well as how past and present connections gel as needed to deal with a crucial situation.

Risk Assessment

How much confidence should you have in your intuition? Having a strong sense that you know something is a sign that your intuition has been at work. The question is, Can you depend on that sense of knowing to be true or correct in your current situation? To evaluate this, you should consider doing a risk assessment.

Professional and personal risk is a concern for just about anyone who is paying attention to the way today's world works. Some organizations have personnel on staff solely to assess the level of risk involved in each activity being considered. Individually, risk is also a big factor to consider when deciding how much we should rely on one of our ideas. Risk is a reality for all of us. We all face the issue of keeping enough chips with our dogs that they will continue to trust us.

Section 21. Final Words

Please Be Clear

In ending this book, I would like to be sure one thing is clear. This book is intended to help build a foundation for a great relationship between humans and dogs. If that foundation is built early, many problems will be prevented.

If problems already exist, this plan becomes the basis upon which we begin problem solving. The foundation we outline becomes the structure upon which additional planning takes place and is evaluated.

A Consistent Teaching Approach

When explaining our approach, I have been meticulous in laying out how we teach. As a dog owner, you need to be so consistent in the way you teach your dog that he can tell when you are trying to start something new because he recognizes your technique.

Nothing Takes Place in a Vacuum

Frequently, I am called upon to explain that a dog's behaviors do not occur in a vacuum; they occur within whatever structure exists in the dog's life. Behaviors are much easier to resolve if they are tackled by first establishing a set of clear parameters and communication cues.

James Akenhead

About the Author

For more than 45 years, Jim has owned and trained a variety of dogs. He and his wife, Dr. Charlene Akenhead, have bred and trained Shepherds and Malamutes for 50 years. In 1995, Jim and his son Matt formed Signature K-9 Training and Behavior LLC in northeastern Ohio. Signature K-9 does about two-thirds of its work in private consultations. About half their work is with difficult dogs. In addition to the usual group classes, they also offer group classes for reactive and shy dogs.

Jim has five earned degrees, including a Doctorate in Research and Education as well as a Masters Degree in Counseling. He is certified as a canine trainer and behavior consultant by four independent organizations. He is listed in seven *Who's Who* anthologies on leadership and has been recognized as a Distinguished Alumni by Bowling Green State University. Along with his wife, Charlene, Jim was chosen as Business and Professional Person of the Year in their community.. In 2009, Jim presented at the conference of the International Association of Animal Behavior Consultants and for the Canine Behavior program at Kutztown University. He frequently presents his views on canine aggression.

Jim is the author of four other books. He is a member of the board of directors for the International Association of Animal Behavior Consultants where he also serves as Human Resource Coordinator. He is also a professional member of the Association of Pet Dog Trainers and the International Association of Canine Professionals.

James Akenhead

Selected References

If you read Section 20, which is about intuition, you know I believe that everything we experience in life can have an effect on our thoughts, values and beliefs. The specific references cited below were mentioned in the text of the book. When I began to list other references that I could say have influenced my learning—some because they taught me what to do, some the opposite—my list was 19 pages long before I decided to stop.

My dilemma became, should I continue to list those who have had an influence on my learning and possibly end up with 40 pages of references (which could increase the price of the book), or should I instead provide a more general thank you to those who have made dog behavior their lives since the 1960s, when I began training?

Some people have suggested that I list some of the best-known writers and behavior professionals to show that I have sought advice from the recognized best. My problem with that approach is that literally hundreds of behavior professionals have contributed to my approach through observing their work and reading their thoughts, and I did not want to list some and not others. Thus, this general note instead.

Please don't implicate others in the things you don't like about my approach. What I have included in this book is my adaptation of a great deal of information that I have digested over the decades and integrated into my own approach. I appreciate the work of all those who have contributed to the body of knowledge that now exists.

* * * * *

Akenhead, James, *Unless You're a Hermit, Success Means Working with People.* CCB Publishing, 2008.

Bailey, Jon and Mary Burch, *How to Think Like a Behavior Analyst.* Lawrence Erlbaum Associates, 2006.

Grandin, Temple and Catherine Johnson, *Animals Make Us Human: Creating the Best Life for Animals.* Houghton Mifflin Harcourt, 2009.

Helmstetter, Shad, Ph.D., *What to Say When You Talk to Yourself.* Simon & Schuster, 1986.

Massey, Morris, Ph.D., *The People Puzzle: Understanding Yourself and Others.* Reston Publishing, 1979 .

Pryor, Karen, *Don't Shoot the Dog! The New Art of Teaching and Training,* 3rd edition. Ringpress Books, 2002.

Scott, John Paul, and John Fuller, *Genetics and the Social Behavior of the Dog.* The University of Chicago Press, 1965.

The Dumb Friends League of Denver, Colorado, was established in 1910 and is dedicated to shelter, education and advocacy for companion animals. You'll find information sheets for dealing with common canine problems on their web site, www.ddfl.org/tips.htm.

The Monroe Institute in Faber, Virginia, is an education and research organization devoted to the exploration of human consciousness. The audio materials mentioned in this book may be found by visiting their web site, www.monroeinstitute.org.

CPSIA information can be obtained at www.ICGtesting.com
Printed in the USA
BVOW080641250613

324205BV00001B/5/P